True Stories of Messages from Beyond

Extraordinary Messages and Signs From Lost Loved Ones

www.messages-from-beyond.com

I.S.B.N. **(13)** 978-0-9746093-7-9
I.S.B.N. **(9)** 0-9746093-7-4

Author: Julie A. Mucha-Aydlott

Cover Photo by: Julie A. Mucha-Aydlott

Cover Graphic Design by: Eva Urick, Urick Design

Published by:

San Diego Business Accounting Solutions
a "Non" CPA Firm
P.O. Box 11128
Lakeside, CA 92040
www.messages-from-beyond.com

Dedication

This one is for you, Mom! My guardian angel, who has countless times given me the comforting signs that you are still with me no matter how far away your spirit soars. Just for the once-in-a-lifetime chance to be your daughter, I would endure all of the pain of missing you. For that is what love is.

Contents

Introduction

No one really knows what heaven looks like, where we go exactly, and if the Bible's perception of the life ever after is how it actually is. One thing I feel for certain, though. Within our earthly bodies are our eternal souls. Whether your belief is of eternal life in heaven, advancing to a higher plane, or non-existence, there are too many encounters with life after death to call them a mere coincidence. Some things just can't be explained by science. I truly believe that the mere existence of our soul is so far out of our conception of what's possible that we won't ever understand until we ourselves pass on. So many people try to rationalize miraculous events to such an extreme that it makes me believe in it even more. I decided to write this book not only to share my stories, but to share the stories of others that I have had the privilege to read.

Beverly

When I was 22, I was diagnosed with cervical cancer. My pap smear came back a class 4. You would think they could come up with a better name for this stuff, but nonetheless, that's what they call the test. After a series of colposkopies, freezing, and three-month followup tests, the cancer would continuously grow back and multiply. I was going through infertility at the time, as well, and was desperately trying to get pregnant because I knew I was in trouble. My doctor had suggested a hysterectomy and I bluntly said no, I want children! My last pap smear during this long 24 months of testing was taken in December of 1994. By the grace of God the cancer had just disappeared. My doctor told me to be very careful, that by the time I turned 30, it would most likely come back.

As time, procrastination and stress would have it, I turned 33; and two beautiful girls, a divorce and a new marriage later, I didn't make time for myself and skipped about two years of check-ups. December 2003 was a stressful end to a year.

Life was beating us up one side and down the other and during all of it, I started getting a lot of abdominal pain as well as my lower limbs going numb. I was scared to death. I made an emergency appointment to get into the doctor and have my annual test that I'd been so graciously missing. My doctor immediately saw lumps around my cervix, as well as swelling. The first thought that came to my mind was that I had waited too long and that the cancer had come back and spread. My deep fear was that instead of cervical cancer, I might have ovarian cancer. The thought of fighting so hard to get my children, now to take the risk of losing them because of foolish procrastination, was too much! I called my mom as soon as I got home. She could hear the terror in my voice, and as all good mothers who love their children do, she said "Oh kiddo, if I could take it from you, I would."

It took two months to get my test results back from the doctor, after going in for additional tests. The time was killing me. The not knowing was enough to drive you mad. Wondering what your future will hold, what should you do, how much you have left undone. I had just got married for the second time on September 19, 2003, to the love of my life. My girls were 8 and 6. When the doctor finally called me to tell me the news, it was more a feeling of amazement than anything else. "We're not quite sure where it went. It seems to have disappeared, and you're fine." Those words were a blessing to my ears. Once again, not a second but a third chance – but there was a huge price to pay.

February of every year my mom Beverly and I would do our annual ritual and meet in Las Vegas for her birthday. Her birthday was February 16th. I hated the fact that I lived in San Diego while she had moved back home to Colorado in 1991. I had wanted to move back home for twenty years now. Let me see, how long have I been in San Diego? That would be twenty years. Unfortunately with a husband who promised to move back home throughout twelve years of a relationship, there was always another excuse why I couldn't move home. After having children, I couldn't take my girls away from their dad, so in essence, he won anyway. Not that San Diego is a bad place to live. I have learned a great deal, met my new husband, and grown so much as a person that I don't regret it, but as Dorothy says, "There's no place like home." My mom and I would plan as many visits as either one could afford at the time so that her granddaughters would get to see her as much as possible, but those Las Vegas trips were such a nice getaway for just the two of us to hang out and spend time together.

Our last trip to Vegas was in February 2004. I remember getting to the hotel before she arrived. I was so excited to see my mom, as I hadn't seen her since the year before. I was sitting in the hotel lobby anxiously waiting for her to walk through the door. When she finally arrived I was taken aback by the woman that I saw walking toward me. Once the best-looking mom, always getting whistles and invitations for dinner, and now this frail, slower and older-looking woman walking through the door. I was too excited to see her to analyze what was different, but in my heart I knew something was terribly wrong. This trip she wasn't as lively, she didn't have a lot of energy and she just felt and looked tired. We would always go to a comedy show and have the best time. This year she tried to laugh, but it looked as though she hurt. During this trip was her 59th birthday.

That night in the hotel room, I couldn't sleep. I got up to use the restroom and saw the lights from the Vegas strip shining through the window. I looked over at my mom sleeping peacefully on her bed and knew in that instant that she was dying. It was a heartbreaking sick feeling that I had never felt before. I went into the bathroom and cried. I tried not to let my emotions or thoughts affect our trip, and I remained happy and just thankful to be there with her. When our trip came to an end, our flights were departing close to the same time. I was able to walk with my mom for quite a while and just soak in this last visit. As her line turned toward the left and mine toward the right, we shared a huge hug goodbye, and I watched her walk off to her waiting area. Both of our flights were delayed for over four hours. We talked to each other on our cell phones until the batteries died.

A few days later, my mom called and left a message on my answering machine that will haunt me forever. Her voice was so different. I had never heard her sound that way in my life. Something was terribly wrong. My sisters had been having issues with my mom at the time, the typical family politics that went unresolved. My mom's message sounded desperate, asking me if I had talked to my sisters and if I could get hold of them. She wanted them to call her.

I called her back as soon as I got home and asked her what was wrong, if everything was okay. She said she was in a lot of pain. Since she got back from Vegas, the pain had hit her so hard. I asked her where the pain was. She said it was on her back between her shoulder blades. She said she had gone to the doctor and had x-rays but they didn't see anything. I asked her if they checked her for lung cancer and she told me the doctor said her lungs were clean. The pain was so unbearable that she was crying. In my entire life, my mom was a very private person and rarely cried in front of anyone. This woman of steel had conquered so many difficult obstacles in her life, but managed to protect us from those hard times that she suffered. I think I have only seen her cry once, at my first wedding when she told me after my divorce that she was crying because I married the spitting image of my dad who died when I was four, which wasn't exactly the right choice. After I hung up the phone with my mom, I looked at my husband crying and I said "I know she has lung cancer."

For the next few months, the pain became so much worse. I would call my mom daily to ask her how she was doing. Sometimes she would be able to answer the phone and talk for just a minute, but most of the time she was trying to rest. This was a woman who had worked just about every day of her life since she was 14.

Everything finally came to a head on May 4th, 2004. My oldest brother had to take my mom to the emergency room because the pain was literally killing her. She had lost twenty pounds in two months, not being able to eat because of the pain.

I was sitting at my desk working when I got the phone call. My brother said that he had taken my mom into the emergency room, and the ER doctor had given her morphine and started taking blood tests and doing cat scans. The mere mention of the word morphine and I exclaimed, "They think she has cancer!" He couldn't believe what I was saying, until ten minutes later when the doctors came in and told him that the test results came back positive for lung cancer. Her tumor was the size of a golf ball, just above her left lung – high enough to be out of view from the x-rays taken a few months back.

With the news of my mom, I rushed home to my husband who was building our dream house. Everything was falling apart, all the way down to building our house. He held me for as long as I could remember. He had just lost his father two years before, to lung cancer as well. Oddly enough, his dad was only 61. I find it an incredible coincidence that the baby boomers between the ages of 57 and 65 are dying from lung cancer. It must be something in the air. Ash from Mount St. Helens circled the globe twice when it erupted in the 80s. Who's to say that the test nuclear bombs set off in Nevada during the 40s didn't do the same thing? Whichever way the wind is blowing!

I remember the suffocating feeling as though something is standing on your chest. In my entire life, the only immediate family member to pass away was my dad, but I was only four years old, so I barely remember when my dad passed away. I had never experienced the feeling of loss of this magnitude. I pulled my girls out of school and jumped on the next available flight to Denver. I wanted to make sure that my mom was able to see her granddaughters, especially without any certainty of whether she would pass immediately, or what was going on.

The plane ride seemed to take forever, and once we landed in Denver I was in a state of shock. I don't even recall how I managed to get from the baggage claim with two kids in tow, to the car rental yard then to Loveland in record time. My girls were very scared, not knowing what to expect when they saw their Grandma.

We got to the hospital at 7:30 on May 4, 2004. I was so nervous, not knowing what to say, but it was still Mom. She was still awake. The girls and I finally found her room, and there she was. My mom was sitting there on the bed, face lit up with a huge smile at the sight of her daughter and granddaughters. She looked the same as in Las Vegas – a bit thinner but she still looked alive. I was so relieved that she was alive. The whole time she was worried that she didn't have enough food in the fridge for us, but invited us to stay at her house. I was so glad to see her and hug her. The girls were excited to see Grandma again. The doctors had her pain under control, but she didn't know when they would release her. She was starting to get a bit tired so the girls and I left for her house so she could get some rest.

Mother's Day was coming up this Sunday. What an unfair Mother's Day present for her. When the girls and I got to her house, it was very warm and inviting. She had painted the walls in the living room a nice shade of mauve. It made it look comfortable, like home. I got the girls something to eat and shoved them off to bed. I sat downstairs and started looking through my mom's photo albums. There were pictures of her as a small child; she was wearing a white communion dress and had to have been about 10. She looked just like Kalie, my oldest daughter. The thought of losing my mom crushed my heart into a billion pieces.

That following morning, we rushed back to the hospital, and as we pulled up to the entrance I noticed my brother Rob wheeling out my mom. They let her out early! This was great news! My head started going into a million different directions, thinking maybe they caught it in time. Maybe she had a chance to fight it. In my head I thought it was time to turn this trip into a memorable visit home and figure out what we could do to save my mom's life.

The girls stayed at best friend Cindy's house and played with her kids while I took my mom to appointments. That's when I met Gina. She was incredible. She was in charge of State Aid for the hospital through a company called Banner Health. We went over finances, what insurance my mom didn't have, her medical bills and how to proceed on applying for State Aid. Between the two of us, anything she asked for she had within hours. We were able to get my mom on Social Security within two months of her diagnosis. She treated my mom like a queen, and we became good friends. Without her help, the illness would have been so much more stressful for my mom.

All of the schedules for chemotherapy and radiology filled up the calendar. The doctors wanted to go after the lump and felt confident that they could keep it at bay. We didn't know if it had spread to any other organs yet, and were waiting for those test results. This is where I vowed to help my mom with anything she needed. On the weekends that my ex-husband would have our girls, I would plan my trips home because I couldn't bring them each time. I saw the beautiful seasons of Colorado come and go from May on. My two biggest hang-ups with California are the fact that you have no clue what time of year it is because there aren't any noticeable seasons so close to the ocean, and there isn't any weather aside from hot and hotter. I love Colorado thunderstorms and of course the snow! Each time I would come home, I would pray that I would get one or the other.

Each trip had its definite memories. One in particular was when my brother Ron had a huge surprise for my mom. Back in the early 80s when my mom was President of the Industrial Banks in Colorado, she bought Monroe Industrial Bank. She had always wanted a Corvette, and having five kids, there isn't much room for groceries or kids. So my mom finally bought herself a 1978 Limited Edition Silver Anniversary Corvette. She loved that car so much. I can't believe she let us drive it. I actually got my drivers license in that car!

As time went on, my brother Ron was trying to get his business off the ground in the mid 90s. My mom gave him her Corvette so that he could obtain more capital for his business. He sold the Corvette and over the next ten years built up a business that was doing very well. When my mom was diagnosed, Ron hired a private investigator to track down the Vette from the VIN number. He found it in Florida and convinced the current owner to sell it to him. My sister Cindy and I were helping Ron to plan this surprise. The trucking company had the car delivered to Denver where we met him to pick it up. There it was in all its glory, the infamous Vette. It looked pretty good considering it had been through so much. The previous owner was trying to restore it, and had quite a bit to go. I hopped in the car and took it for a spin around the block. It was so weird. You could even feel how the seat tilted like before; everything was still the same in the old Vetter, as my mom called it.

On the way back to Loveland, Cindy and I stopped at a party shop and picked up a gigantic bow and some balloons. When we got home, Mom was still sleeping. We were trying to time it just perfectly. We had it pulled on the lawn with ribbon and balloons all over the place. We went inside her house and anxiously waited for her to wake up. We called Ron who was still in New Mexico and told him everything was ready. He was going to call Mom in about fifteen minutes when we expected her to get up. We called our Aunt Barb and told her to get over to Mom's as soon as possible, that Ron had a surprise for her.

My mom finally got out of bed and headed down the stairs. She was in a bit of pain, but Cindy and I were sitting there with a s---t eating grin on our face, and the phone rang. The timing was perfect; it was Ron. I answered it and said "Mom, Ron needs to talk to you." Cindy went outside to turn on the camcorder. I got up and got my camcorder and started recording. I'm not sure what Ron said to her on the phone, but she slowly stood up, started crying, and walked towards the front door. I can remember it like it was yesterday. She stood at the screen door with tears flowing down her cheek saying, "Oh my God, the Vetter."

She knew it wasn't a replacement Vette; it was her Vette, the one she had picked out and bought. She walked outside so thrilled and shocked. She opened the car door and sat in the Vette; she looked so natural in that car. She took it for a little spin around the block, and it was so nice to see her glowing. She was fighting the worst battle in her life and I knew it wasn't a winning one.

I was able to bring the girls back again in July for a week. We were able to make it into a nice vacation. They went up the Big Thompson Canyon and camped out with their Uncle Ron while I took mom to chemo and radiology. After dealing with all of the medical information, having been given all forms of power of attorney, I was receiving the copies of documentation for Social Security purposes. I was having wishful thinking too. I wanted the treatment to work, but I knew from what the doctors had written that stage 4 small-cell lung cancer was not curable. The last records showed that the cancer had spread to my mom's bones and liver. Was it worth all of the days and nights of vomiting? Or the pain of not being able to swallow because your throat was burned so badly from the radiology? I could only imagine the hell she was going through.

My trips gave her something to look forward to. Every time I would come back, I would have a different car. Sometimes a Mustang, sometimes a Cadillac, even a PT Cruiser once. One trip to chemo I remember my mom sitting in the car, and we were yapping about everything, and I just came out and asked her, "Mom, you remember when you said you would take the cancer from me if you could? What did you do?" She looked at me and said, "I don't know; weird, isn't it."

She was such a strong woman. I wanted to be just like her. On October 14, 2004, we celebrated my 34th birthday. She wanted to buy me a cake and even candles, so we went to the store and she bought me a birthday cake. My Aunt Barb, sister Cindy and nephew Tommy came over to sing happy birthday to me with my mom. I could see how happy it made her. She knew and I knew this would be the last birthday I would celebrate with her. I could see her eyes glow with happiness, knowing how much pain she was in, but she wanted to celebrate with me. It made me happy, sad and angry all at the same time. Why did it need to be this way? How could you celebrate life when you know you're dying? To pretend to be happy, but to play mind games with mortality, coping with the inevitable. But she was happy I was there, and so was I. As soon as I got home to San Diego, wouldn't you know it, my mom called to tell me it had snowed.

I made it out for Thanksgiving, but the girls stayed at their dad's house. Chris had his hands full with the house, and even though he is the General Contractor, it doesn't mean that we don't go through all of the B.S. that everyone else has to. Our framer decided to leave the job only 80% complete because he had a bigger name on the other line. With all the years it never rains in Southern California, this time it started in October. Wouldn't you know it, the day after my husband loaded drywall in the house, it rained! A good 10% of the sheets were ruined.

I spent Thanksgiving trying to cook my mom's special potato dumplings and kraut. I would always botch it. Somehow I couldn't seem to get it right, but this time I did a pretty good job. Everyone came over except my sister Sandi. The snow and bad weather ended up in Colorado Springs, so she couldn't get out.

My mom's pain started to get much worse. After dinner she went up to her room to get away from all of the noise. My nephew Tommy came downstairs to get me and said Grandma needed me. I went up to my mom's room and she was sitting on the side of her bed in excruciating pain. She told me she forgot to take her Percocet and the pain got away from her. She didn't want anyone else to know, so I went downstairs, grabbed her pain meds and hurried back upstairs without anyone seeing me. After everyone left the house, I finished cleaning up the piles of dishes and made an extra plate for my mom. She hadn't been eating much so I wanted to make sure there was something easy for her to grab when she woke up.

I thumbed through the little Thomas Kincaid notebook that I got for her and read some of her entries. Every time I would leave to go back home, there would be an entry from my mom with a sad face saying she was sad I had to leave. Then when I would be showing up, she would have an excitement in her entry saying, "Julie's coming today!" It made me feel so good to know she really looked forward to my visits, but it also made me sad to know I couldn't stay. Just like every other trip, I had to leave on this one too. And of course, that storm that got my sister in the Springs, hit Loveland the following night, after I left. When I got home to San Diego, there was yet another message from my mom letting me know the airport had briefly shut down and that there was a blizzard with 8-foot snow drifts! Someone upstairs has a sick sense of humor.

The first part of January 2005 my mom seemed to be okay, still having a great deal of pain but coping with it as best she could. Because she didn't want another chemo session before she took her trip with Cindy and Ron to Mexico in December, the doctors had it scheduled for the beginning of January when she returned. This one didn't go well at all. It was like opening the flood gates. It completely knocked her down not only physically, but mentally. I think through everything I had emotionally struggled with since my mom's diagnosis, this trip home was the most devastating and difficult event in my life. My Aunt Barb called me at work, frantic. My mom had been violently vomiting since the chemo session a few days prior. She was sure that it was time. She thought my mom was going to pass.

I made my fourteenth trip to Colorado that day. When I got there, my mom looked different, so sad and confused. She told me she was scared to death because she couldn't control her thoughts and she wasn't able to have one positive thought. We sat hugging and talking about how she was feeling. She didn't want to die. It was so hard to listen to her tell me that she wished she would have never found out that she had cancer. Her mortality was really hitting her hard. The pain was so excruciating, I couldn't even begin to know how much pain she was in. She never complained or, as she called it, had a pity party, but just said that she couldn't control her thoughts. For my mom, not being able to be in charge of herself was not an option, but this time she didn't have a choice.

I had to ask my mom the hardest question in the world. It was like saying "Mom, are you ready to die?" I looked at my mom, tears flowing down my cheeks, and I said "Mom, do you want me to call hospice?" Oh my God, I had to say it and do it! It's ironic because I'm the baby, my mom was the baby of her family too, and just like her, the responsibility was mine. She looked at me with her beautiful blue eyes and said "Yes, maybe they could help me get out of this depression that I can't control." She knew how I was feeling and she was such an incredible person. She told me that she wouldn't have chosen anyone else to handle everything and that I was just like her. That was the biggest compliment in the world, but in the process it made me age another twenty years.

I finally confided in my mom something I thought I would never let her know. When the doctors initially diagnosed her and gave her treatment options, they never told her how long she would have. In the beginning, she really thought that the chemo and radiation would prolong the cancer for at least a few years. Because I had to handle all of the disability insurance and hospital information, I knew in May that she only had nine months at the most. I told her what was written on her medical records that I had to submit to Social Security. From her reaction, she had felt it in her heart even though she didn't hear it firsthand. I was relieved that I told her what I knew, and my mom, being who she is, had to say, "You carried this around all this time, you poor kid." So as we sat there on her couch holding hands, I dialed the phone and set up the appointment for the following day.

The whole morning didn't seem real. There was a numbing detached feeling about the entire thing. You know you have to do it, it tears your heart apart, but you sit there thinking, who the hell am I to complain, my mom is dying of cancer. Just suck it up and take charge!

My brother was flying in from New Mexico and my other sister was coming down from Colorado Springs. My mom didn't want everyone to know she had cancer, but the last person she wanted to see was her brother Larry. He also made an emergency trip from Omaha. Everyone was to meet the following day. My mom, so worried about me all the time, wanted me to get out and not be locked up in her house all day while she was sleeping. She was sleeping so much. We decided that I would go up to Fort Collins to see my sister Cindy.

I was exhausted from all of the emotional stress, and Cindy and I stayed up talking about everything and anything. I felt the guilt of laughing, of crying, and was just feeling beat. I think the laughing part was the best medicine. Leave it to my sister Cindy – she should have been a comedian –

but she is also just as emotional as I am. If I were a fly on the wall in her house, I would have thought those two were completely nuts.

Early the following morning I left my sister's house and headed back down to Loveland. I needed to stop and get something to eat. I hadn't eaten anything substantial in months. I needed strength for the appointment with hospice. I stopped in to the local Loveland Lake Restaurant and tried my damnedest to sit at a booth and look normal. My coffee was the only thing that I could taste. I tried to eat, but the hot bowl of oatmeal sat there and got cold. I couldn't keep the tears from streaming down my face. It was horrible. All I could think of was hospice. I had to call hospice because my mom was dying. People in the restaurant kept looking at me. I imagine I looked pretty sad. I kept turning my head toward the wall so no one could see my pain, but everyone in that room felt it with me. It was so weird.

This nice little old lady in a bright red sweater sat down next to me in the booth and just hugged me. She had no clue why I was crying or who I was, but she loved me just because. The words came shaking from my mouth; I told her that I had to call hospice for my mom, that she was dying. The lady cried with me. After she said she would say a prayer for my mom, she got up and left. The next thing I knew there was another young lady who was with her boyfriend, and she gave me a hug too as she was walking towards the cashier. No wonder why I miss Loveland Colorado so much. It was therapeutic. It was like they took some of my pain so I could continue with what I needed to do. They were a blessing for me. I guess, thus the name "Loveland."

The waitress was so nice too. She was trying not to pry, but overheard my conversation and told me she had just found out the week before that she had breast cancer. It was everywhere. Not just me. I didn't know how to react or what to say except my best wishes and prayers are with you. I left a twenty on the table and headed towards the restroom. I didn't want my mom to see the mascara marks down my face, so I tried to wash it off. I decided some nice cold Colorado air would help hide the red eyes. I headed out of the restaurant and started to drive away when the waitress came running out to give me my change. A bowl of oatmeal and a coffee don't add up to much. I told her the change was for her, so she got teary-eyed and said, "Thank you so much." It was the least I could do, for how much pain they took from me.

I headed towards Loveland Lake and found a nice picnic area where I just stood there staring at the frozen lake and the already fallen snow. It was hypnotic. So many things flooded my mind: my mom, hospice, the house, my girls, life, death, non-existence and eternal life. Where do we go, what does all of it mean? It was too much to digest. I was so lost in thought that I stood there in the freezing temperature for over an hour. Then in a panic, I headed back to my mom's house because I didn't want to miss any more precious time with her.

I was able to hang out with my mom for a few hours before all the "fam damily" arrived. My mom was also a very funny sarcastic person so I am using some of her trademark expressions in this book. Then Ron, Aunt Barb, Rob, Sandi, Cindy, and

Tommy were all there with me waiting for the hospice nurse to arrive. When she arrived, you could have cut the air. Everyone was in shock and not sure what to expect. My mom, trying to keep a smile on her face, sat on the couch with her tired little body and started answering the toughest questions. "What kind of funeral do you want? Do you want to be cremated or buried? What funeral home is the best choice? How bad is your pain"? Then she started asking all of the technical questions, "What types of treatments have you finished, who is your doctor, what medications are you on? How many assets do you have? Who are all of your children, their spouses, and any other family? Can they be contacted? How can you pay hospice, will you need assistance?" Everyone has a responsibility in this world, and mine was to answer all of these questions because I was the only one who really knew. Cindy and Barb had taken care of my mom, bringing dinner, picking up medicines and taking her to doctor visits. But during the nine-month period, I had helped her schedule chemo, sat with her on her first session, took her to radiology a dozen times and sat in the waiting room, and handled all of the paperwork.

I could tell the appointment was taking its toll on my mom. The next question brought my mom to tears. "How are you feeling right now"? This time she couldn't control the stream of tears flowing down her face. She said "I am just so depressed, I can't think positive, I just want it to end." She looked at all of us and said she was tired, she needed to go upstairs for a few minutes. We finished the appointment with hospice and got the schedule on how frequently the nurses would come and check my mom's vitals and ability to continue to stay at home. The appointment was finally over. I don't know how these men and women can go from house to house caring for dying people. God bless them. Each day dealing with grieving families, family politics, and comforting the dying. I don't know if I could ever do it.

The following day, my Uncle Larry showed up at the house and was finally able to visit with my mom. We gave them some one-on-one time because they hadn't seen each other in a few years. Everyone planned on coming back later and bringing food for a potluck. It was a nice evening; everyone seemed to get along, and my brother Ron showered my mom with more gifts. She had an enormous stack of DVDs to keep her occupied, lots of old movies, the ones she really likes. She felt like a queen again. It started to get late and I remember looking at my Aunt Barb and Uncle Larry wishing they would go back to my Aunt's house because my flight left the next day and this would be my last night with my mom. As great minds think alike – not that she didn't enjoy spending time with her brother and sister – she was thinking the same thing.

We sat up pretty late talking and sharing our last night together. It was so tough. I knew she was hurting pretty bad, but she knew as well as I did that this would be our last night together. I wanted to stay longer; I knew if I left that I would never see her again, not coherent. I had to leave, though; my girls couldn't stay at their dad's that long, as I knew he was making really bad choices and I didn't trust his behavior and priorities through all of this. I could barely sleep. My mom was up quite a bit vomiting and I felt so helpless. The agonizing feeling of pain and suffering that she was going through just didn't seem fair.

I finally got out of bed about 6:30 a.m. and started getting ready to go to the airport. I did everything I possibly could to keep back the tears. Packing my suitcase was so hard. I walked down the stairs and my mom was sitting on the couch looking just as disappointed as I was. I cried hugging her and holding her, telling her I would be back in a few weeks: "I promise, Mom!" I kept telling her, "Don't worry I'll be back!" I loaded the car, and pulled out of the driveway knowing that was the last time I would see my mom standing in the door waving goodbye to me. She was crying too. We both knew, this was it; if I made it back in a few weeks, everything would be different. I never cried so hard in my life. I could barely see the road driving to the airport. I believe that leaving that morning was the hardest thing I have ever had to do in my life. I had to go, with my mom standing there alive, still able to communicate, and I wouldn't ever get to see her like that again. This is where the phrase was invented, "Life sucks and then you die."

Of course, wouldn't you know it, the next morning my mom calls me to let me know I missed the snow, AGAIN! I guess I was just not meant to see it snow anymore!

Sunday, February 13th, 2005 was not a normal day by any means. My husband only had two days to get our certificate of occupancy signed off on our house before the lender penalized us for not finishing on time. The stress level was enormous. The inside of the house was not finished, with flooring, countertops and mainly finish work yet to do. We were already significantly short with the costs to finish, and everything seemed to be crashing hard. My mom's birthday was in three days; it was to be her 60th birthday.

The phone conversations started becoming shorter and shorter. She didn't have the energy to talk on the phone and would normally just let me know she was doing fine. Today it was different. My brother Rob dialed the phone for her and her voice was so distant. It was so frightening that I really don't know how to explain it. It was like she was half gone. She kept calling my name but couldn't hear me talking. Tears streaming down my face, I'm trying desperately not to let her hear how terrified I am. It was time, she was dying and there wasn't a damn thing I could do to stop it. She didn't want to hang up the phone, and just kept calling my name, saying "Julie, are you still there"? My heart was beating so fast I thought it was going to jump out of my chest. I told my mom, "Please wait for me, I'll make it back, I promise, I promise I will be there!" After I hung up the phone I fell to my knees crying hysterically. I felt guilty as hell for asking her to wait for me, considering how much pain she was in. I didn't want her to go, I wanted to hug her and hold her hand, but I was so far away.

The morning of Valentine's Day was my nightmare starting bright and early. My sister Cindy called me and told me that hospice had the ambulance come and take my mom to the hospital. They said she had a day, two at the most. While I was trying frantically to get on the next flight out of San Diego, my husband's hell was burning all around.   The utility company and the fire department both had appointments to sign off on the house that day. The rent-an-inspector from the fire department had an attitude before she even stepped on the property. She couldn't tell the difference between dirt and asphalt and refused to sign off on our house. They forced us to put in a circular driveway before they would sign off, even though we had the main driveway in. The utility company said our utility closet was twelve inches too short. They had plans and drawings already approved for twelve months. They apparently don't read them just so they can make you tear half your wall off and pull it out another twelve inches, or maybe it's because department A has nothing to do with department B. These people were creating such a crisis in my life I realized how insignificant all of this was.

One more thing and I thought that would be it, I would have a meltdown, but I didn't. Neither did my husband. He loaded up his truck with my suitcase, and I made sure I packed the VHS recording of the last share day Kalie had at school.

In January she sang the song "Hero" by Mariah Carey for Grandma. I was going to bring it with me my next trip. God, I didn't want to bring it on my last!

On the way to the airport, I stopped into my girls' school to tell them it was time and I had to go home because Grandma was getting ready to go to heaven. Kalie is as emotional as I am and didn't take it too well. I can see her eyes filling with tears as I'm typing this now. She kept saying "No, I don't want her to go"! It was so painful to hear her pain. Emily, still being young enough not to really understand, gave me a big hug and told me to tell Grandma she loved her. I hugged them as tight as I possibly could. At the airport, my husband hugged me as tight as he possibly could. He couldn't come with me, with everything falling apart, and he felt guilty for me going by myself, but it was okay. I knew it was okay.

The flight attendants were very compassionate. They made sure I had a seat up front so I could be the first one off the plane. I remember the feeling of rush, rush, rush. Hurry or

I'm going to be too late. The flight seemed to take forever, and once again I was completely lost in my thoughts of being too late. I was looking out the window of the plane; it had already started to get dark, and I felt a sense of peace and reassurance. I knew she wasn't gone yet and I still had time to see her. It was like she was telling me to slow down, that I would make it in time.

I got to the hospital a little after midnight of Valentine's Day. I rushed to my mom's room and saw her lying there, peacefully sleeping. I sat beside her bed and held her hand; it was still warm. She squeezed my hand, letting me know she knew I made it. I promised I would, and she waited. God I didn't want her to die. Her birthday was in just one more day. My sister Cindy was sleeping on a small cot next to my mom's bed. My brother Ron walked in the room and told me there wasn't much I could do here tonight and kidnapped me. He let me stay the night in his hotel suite. The bed was very comfortable, enough to let me get some sleep, but I still woke up frequently.

February 15th, 2005, a day I will never forget. It was about 7:00 in the morning when I woke up in a panic – not realizing that if something happened with my mom at the hospital, the nurses would have called. I finally settled down a bit and took a shower. I got ready as quickly as I could and told my brother I would meet him in the banquet room, that I needed coffee.

When I left the room and started walking towards the elevator, that's when I saw them! There was an enormous window looking out to the courtyard; I couldn't believe my eyes. It was snowing! The biggest, fluffiest Christmas snowflakes I had ever seen in my life! In all my years I have never seen a more beautiful snowfall than on this morning. It was my mom! She gave me the snow! While I stood there in absolute amazement watching these huge Christmas snowflakes fall from the sky, I told my mom thank you for the beautiful gift and that today was a perfect day for her to go to her next journey. As painful as it was to let go, she needed all of us to let go so she could leave in peace.

The snow kept coming down all day as if by magic. The world keeps turning as life continues on for everyone around you and you often wonder if they know the pain you are feeling inside. I didn't want to take any chances of not being with her in case she passed. Not knowing what to expect, but knowing it is right there, just waiting for that specific moment in time to cease to exist. I was happy for her to finally be rid of the pain, but selfish in that I didn't want to let her go.

I sat beside her bed, watching her, holding her hand and telling her I loved her so much, hoping she was not hurting anymore. She was on so much morphine that she was pretty much incoherent. She would groan occasionally from the pain, but for the most part it just looked like she was sleeping. We would all take turns staying with her, and when I slipped out for a few minutes I went downstairs to the billing office to see my friend Gina and to let her know it was time. She had been such a Godsend through this; I was so glad to find a new friend in her.

Sandi was not in yet from Colorado Springs, and my brother Rob didn't get off work until 4:00 or so. I had forgotten my tape of Kalie in the hotel room and asked Ron to hurry back to the hotel and get it for me. When everyone was finally there in my moms' hospital room, I put the tape in of Kalie singing the song "Hero." Here is a little 10-year-old singing her heart out for her grandma at her school's share day. We were all crying because of what it meant to us. I looked at my mom as I was listening to the words of the song, and I saw a tear stream down her face. I knew at that moment that she heard it too. The last song my mom heard was her granddaughter singing for her. It was such a wonderful moment.

About 40 minutes later, everyone was getting up to head out and get something to eat. My aunt had left to go home for a while and rest. Cindy noticed my mom breathing funny and called everyone back into the room. In all my life, I have never seen or experienced anything of this magnitude. It wasn't peaceful like everyone claims. It was so sad and horrible at the same time. She was gasping for air, her eyes tightly closed. It was like she was suffocating. I wasn't expecting it to be like this. Cindy was holding her hand, I was touching her leg, Ron was standing at the foot of the bed and Rob and Sandi were on the other side of the bed, and my nephew Tommy was standing next to Ron. I'm sure my mom was waiting just long enough for my aunt to leave, because my mom didn't feel she could handle it at age 72. We were telling her in hysteria that it's okay, we'll all be okay. "You can go now, Mom." We kept telling her she could go, it was okay to go.

Suddenly the breathing stopped, and there wasn't any more gasping for air. We all thought it was over, but a few seconds later my mom forced her eyes open, her lips clenched together like she was pushing as hard as she could to open her eyes, and she looked at Cindy, Ron and then me, and then just like that she was gone. It was like she wanted to take one more picture of us with her before she left. Just like that, she was gone. I remember standing there looking at her, and crying, feeling her warmth start to turn cold, in complete shock and disbelief.

I'm glad I was there to be with her, but by the same token, it was so tough to watch her die. I actually watched her die.

We asked the nurse if the hospital pastor could come and pray before my mom went to the funeral home. He was in the middle of dinner, so we decided to go and get a bite to eat and come back at 8:00. On the way down the hall, I had to stop into the nurse's station. I sat there all by myself, watching my family walk down the hall as I was discussing moving my mom's body, signing paperwork and handling her plans. I had to turn off the scared little girl crying hysterically, in favor of the professional who could handle all this responsibility. I was doing it for you, Mom; you deserve the best.

The guilt one feels after a sense of relief is enormous. For nine months we have struggled with the thought of losing our mom, with taking care of her, watching her in so much pain, and watching her die. When it is all over you collapse in pure exhaustion but you know that you don't have to do it anymore. The hardest part is over, now it's time to call everyone and plan for a funeral.

I called my cousin Lisa in Omaha. I told her that it happened, my mom passed away. She knew something was wrong with my mom, but I told her that my mom didn't want anyone to know, so I couldn't tell her exactly what. This didn't go over really well with the rest of the family, though. Everyone wanted to be able to see my mom again before she died. They were all in shock and couldn't even believe that she was so sick. My mom didn't want a house full of people just staring at her, as sick as she was. She just wanted immediate family to be around. I asked Lisa to call everyone else for me. I just wasn't up to it. I let her be the life line. I called my best friend Cindy who also lived in Loveland and asked her for her help. She is such a wonderful friend, and in an instant she made herself available for me.

My mom was taken to Kibbey's Funeral Home. It was the same place my dad was 30 years ago. I had an appointment at 10:00 in the morning on her birthday. She passed away just 4 hours before her 60th birthday. We think she did it on purpose so she wouldn't have been considered elderly. When I walked through the front door at Kibbey's, I was the first one there. I had a flood of flashbacks, seeing my dad's coffin right there, in the front room. I remember seeing him in there stiff; he looked scary. I was only 4 and he died of diabetes at the young age of 31. Apparently when I saw my dad lying there I looked at my grandma and said "Give him a candy bar, he'll wake up." Now it was my mom.

She wanted to be cremated, so I asked the funeral home not to cremate her until we could say goodbye one last time. They were very pleasant and helpful. I started going through all of the paperwork with the director and the rest of the family finally showed up. Next, Family Politics 101 (I'm leaving most of it out because that's not the purpose of this book!). They were all upset with me because I was inside already. As my mom would say, "What, are you flippin nuts, I'm not waiting outside, it's 20 degrees out there." Funny how much I love and miss the snow, but stick someone in San Diego for 20 years and the cold weather isn't the same.

We decided to have a memorial service at my sister Cindy's church in Fort Collins. There was a beautiful blue urn with doves flying on the outside. It came with a set of six small urns that matched. Since everyone wanted to have something, I went ahead and ordered the whole set. That way each one of us five kids and my nephew Tommy could all have part of my mom where we lived, then we could spread the remainder of her ashes above the Rocky Mountains, just like she wanted. It was so difficult to be the one who needed to sign the authorization for the funeral home to cremate my mom. I sat there at the table looking at all of my brothers and sisters, wanting to make sure everything was exactly the way my mom wanted it. My mind flashed back to the day I was sitting on her couch holding her hand, asking her if we should call hospice, and her saying she wouldn't want anyone else to handle everything. This was everything. It really takes your breath away, she was here just a day ago, but now she is gone, only to be fond memories and ashes.

After all of the planning was said and done, we were taken to the back room where my mom was lying. It is the most amazing thing to see your loved one lying there empty and lifeless. It is so unreal. It is like a bad dream where you are screaming for them to wake up. She was once this incredibly beautiful, vibrant, extremely intelligent woman, and then she became devastated by cancer. Her little body was so frail and gray, she looked like she was 80 years old. I bent over to kiss her forehead. It was cold and hard. She wasn't in there anymore. I wondered where she was. I know she is somewhere out there, and I truly believe that she will let me know. As I walked out of Kibbey's, I made the appointment with the director to pick up my mom's ashes the following day for the service.

The Corvette was still sitting at the hospital. The brake pedal was pushed all the way to the floor. Cindy and I thought it would be really cool to have the Vette parked on the sidewalk in front of the church with a beautiful spray of roses on the hood and a picture of my mom in the middle. There wouldn't be a person in Fort Collins who wouldn't recognize that car and associate it with my mom.

Ron, Cindy and I decided to go to my mom's house and gather a few personal mementos and then let Rob and Sandi handle the rest. Going there was so difficult. Mom wasn't there standing in the doorway, she wasn't sitting on the couch, but Chemo her kitty was very sad. Cindy took Chemo home with her to stay. In my mom's room, I found this God-awful jewelry box that I made in 7th grade. My mom saved it all this time. It was the first and last thing that I have ever sewn in my life, but it was sitting up in her closet. She wanted Kalie and Emily to have some of her necklaces and rings. It is so hard looking at her stuff. It is her personal things, and she will never get to touch them or use them again. Her nightgown, still lying on her bed waiting for her to put on. Her brush, makeup and her purse. The little things that you never really realize mean so much, but are so difficult to look at when the person is gone.

Ron wanted to be able to have a place to go where mom's name was engraved, and because she wanted to be cremated this didn't leave much of an option. My mom did own a plot right above my dad at Resthaven Cemetery. Ron thought it would be good if we could put some of her favorite things in it, along with the urn after her ashes were scattered. She wouldn't be buried there, it would be just a place to go where some of her items are stored.

I pulled down her beautiful dress, shoes and hat that Ron bought her in Reno. There was a purse that matched so I pulled out her driver's license, some gum, a tissue and her cigarette box. I put one cigarette in it for her. At first glance that may sound a little weird, especially because it is the very thing that killed her, but she would have wanted one. I think we were all pretty emotionally drained at this point, and it was time to go. I loaded up all of the pictures so that we could make a collage for the service, and Cindy and I went to the hospital to pick up the Vette.

That poor car had been through five teenagers, a few new owners and an accident. No wonder it wasn't feeling good. The feeling of not being able to stop was pretty scary. I would have to pump the brakes a good quarter-mile before a stop sign or a stop light in order to come to a complete stop. Loveland to Fort Collins had a lot of traffic and many stop lights. My sister was driving her car in front of me, and there were so many times that I can't believe I didn't hit her. By the time we got to the auto repair shop, I was thanking God that I made it. Even the mechanic said the brakes should have completely gone out the first few stop lights. It was a good 15 miles of stop and go, and someone was looking out for me. I'm pretty sure it was Mom. That night, I tried to finish my elegy. It's not easy writing when you're crying so much, but I was happy with what I had on paper.

The morning of the service, Cindy and I hurried to the church early to set up the flowers and urn. The Corvette was finished in time and Tommy took it to get cleaned. It looked sharp, and Pastor McDermott was kind enough to let us park it out front where everyone could see. Flowers started arriving from people who couldn't make it, and the anxiousness was hitting us. About an hour later, I saw the caravan of mini-vans carrying the Mucha

Clan from Omaha. It was so nice to see all of them, and to know that they cared enough for my mom to come to her funeral, especially since they are all on my dad's side of the family. Everyone was showing up. Old faces that I haven't seen for years, and most of them acting like they had seen a ghost, because Cindy looks so much like my mom that everyone had to do a double-take. There were hugs, and tears, and laughs. Just as Cindy and I suspected, everyone found the church with ease because of the Corvette sitting out front. That car hasn't been around for over 10 years, but everyone still remembers my mom and the Vette.

The service started off beautifully. Cindy sang "Wind beneath my wings," and there wasn't a dry eye in the house. All of us kids took turns going up and speaking on my mom's behalf. Tommy started first, and boy, was that hard. I thought of the girls at home feeling confused, sad and alone. Their mommy wasn't there to comfort them. I'll never forget what Kalie said when I called her to tell her that Grandma was finally in heaven with God. She cried for me, saying, "You don't have a mommy or daddy anymore." No I don't, do I?

When it was my turn to stand up at the podium, I actually didn't feel one ounce of nerves. It was unlike any speech I had ever given. The tunnel vision was something else. I began speaking to all of my mom's friends and our family. I would look up and see tears as I spoke these words:

"One of the many amazing attributes that my mom had was her constant unselfish and giving nature. The most incredible, intelligent and beautiful woman, I was always so amazed by her strength. I always wanted to be just like her, and wanted her to be proud of me. Everyone who knows me knows how much Colorado has meant to me, and not being able to move back home, my mom was my home. My girls and I wrote a little poem book a few years ago called "My favorite time of Year" and dedicated it to my mom. Of course our favorite time is Christmas and Winter. A snow-filled Christmas was such a magical day, and my mom always made Christmas every bit of giving and family that the celebration was meant to be. The last season of the book was "Winter," and said, "But my

favorite time of the year, Christmas! It's finally here! The First snow is always so fluffy and white, so pretty it glimmers and shines really bright."

The flight in to Denver I was feeling like I was racing a clock to see my mom and hold her hand for one last time. By the time the plane took off, I had an overwhelming sense of peace and knew she was waiting for me and my brothers and sisters. I arrived after midnight and my mom squeezed my hand; she knew I made it. My brother Ron kidnapped me because he didn't want me to sleep on a couch at the hospital and I went back to his hotel. I woke up early to hurry back to the hospital to see my mom and as I was walking from the hotel room, the full-length window captured a picture of the most beautiful big fluffy Christmas snowflakes that I have ever seen in my life. My mom gave me the snow that I've been missing each trip I've made out. I had peace with the knowledge that my mom picked today to begin a new journey with God. I don't remember seeing a more beautiful day in my life. It was straight out of a Normal Rockwell painting. The magical gift that my mom gave to me the day she died is once again a sign of her unselfish giving nature.

I've been having a difficult time dealing with the finality of death, and after many have expressed their condolences for our loss of our mom, I wrote this quote for my mom.

"Death is not to lose a loved one, but to find them again after our own journey ends." I will find my mom again, but until then, I will miss her every day."

The service was beautiful. Everyone reminisced about my mom, life, not seeing family except at funerals and weddings, and of course we all promised that we wouldn't just make it on those occasions. I was tired, ready to go home and sleep for a good week. We cleared the reception hall and carried some of the flowers down to my dad's grave. Now it was time for everyone to go about their life. It seemed all of our lives were chaotic. I needed to desperately get hold of mine and get everything under control.

On my trip home, I clipped a few of the beautiful roses to take with me. It was February 21st and I was completely numb. I'll never forget this lady sitting next to me on my flight. She felt terrible, and had absolutely no clue, but the flowers had wilted and looked dead. She said, "Looks like your flowers need some water; they're not doing too well." I turned to her with tears in my eyes, and said, "They are from my mom's funeral. I just wanted to take some home with me." I felt so bad for her; she didn't know, nor did I take any offense to it.

I was relieved and excited to see my husband. He got me home and I clipped the bottom of my dead roses and put them in water. The next morning they amazingly looked brand new and beautiful. They came back to life and lasted for another week. When I was unpacking my suitcase, I came across the perforated boarding pass, and stared at it remembering why it was there. I had to do a double-take. I realized that the boarding pass that I was looking at was dated February 21, 2004, not February 21, 2005. It was the day my mom and I returned from Las Vegas exactly one year before. What are the flippin odds of that happening again?

That night was the first night that I slept soundly in months. I think my body just gave in to pure exhaustion. The next night when I climbed into bed, I remember being in the realm between consciousness and sleep. It was so real. My mom came into my bedroom and sat down at the end of my bed. It was like she was really there. It felt so real; she said, "Hi Kiddo, I just wanted to say thank you for everything you have done for me. It really meant so much." She gave me a big hug. It lasted for a long time. She looked at me and said "I need to go now, I'll see you later," and she was gone. It was so un-dream like, it was real. I truly believe that when someone passes, the best means of communication is through our dream state. It's the only time we have almost all complete un-interruption.

March 23, 2005 was a dreary and awful day. The house wasn't done and we were still short over $70,000 but finally got our Certificate of Occupancy, though we didn't have flooring. I remember waking up not wanting to do this anymore. Why did life need to kick you in your butt so hard all the time? Is there ever a day when things can go good? The rain was coming down in buckets. Sick and tired of the doom and gloom, I drove the girls to school, trying to smile for them. I needed to stop at the bank before I went to the office. As I was pulling out of the Wells Fargo on Fletcher Parkway, I looked up at the dark black and gray clouded sky and saw a ray of sunlight peeking through. It looked like God was shining down from heaven. I instantly thought of my mom, and tears filled my eyes. I said to myself out loud, "Mom, where are you at?" Not a second later the Radio Station KYXY started playing "Hero" by Mariah Carey. I sat there in complete awe realizing that my mom did hear Kalie sing the song; it was way more than any coincidence for the sky, the moment, and the song to occur all at once. My mom was letting me know she's there and that she's okay. Most of all she was letting me know that I was going to be okay too. I cried for almost two hours, and from that moment forward I felt a sense of peace. The bad wasn't so bad, and positive things started happening.

March 23rd was definitely a turning point for me. The pain of losing my mom was still very raw, but I felt such a comfort with the knowledge of the continued existence of my mom. There is no other way to explain it, other than that. She wanted me to accept things as they are and move on with my life. In order to do that, she gave me the biggest message from above, that was just between the two of us.

Her energy is still all around me. I have had an amazing past year. We finally finished our house and moved in on May 14th, 2005. My accounting books have been doing really well and the girls are happy and healthy.

Over the fourth of July, the girls and I flew back to Colorado to have a small memorial service for my mom. My brother Ron rented a plane that would scatter her ashes above the Rocky Mountains and we would place her belongings into the tomb right above my dad. It was a very private family affair. Ron had a company bring in five white doves representing all of us kids saying goodbye to our mom. As the man let the doves fly off, they separated as they flew into the sky. It was as if all of us kids had to go on with our separate lives, and it was okay.

The tomb was opened, and covered with a velvet blanket so that you couldn't see in. My dad's space was on the bottom, and my mom's items were to be placed on the top. The director asked if anyone wished to place the items into the tomb. I of course volunteered. I really didn't know what to expect, but as I kneeled on the grass I picked up my mom's outfit and her purse, and the director pulled the velvet blanket back. My eyes instantly glanced down where I saw my dad's coffin. It was so weird to see it. He was actually in there all this time. It smelled very musty and the air was very thick. It actually scared me to see his coffin. I felt the curiosity of knowing it's in there, wanting to see it and look . . . but once you do you wish you didn't. The only way to get myself through the weird feeling was to say hello to my dad. Then I placed my mom's belongings on a sheet of plywood that separated the bottom level of the tomb from the top. I turned around and gently picked up the blue urn and placed it in front of her purse. "Goodbye Mom, I love you."

Just as I finished, it started to rain. I stood up and looked at Kalie and Emily who were holding on to their Aunt Cindy and Cousin Tommy, and crying.

Because I didn't want them to feel the pain of being there for my mom's actual death, they never got to say goodbye, and I thought it might be easier for them to be there for a beautiful memorial service. It was still very difficult for both of them because they had never experienced a funeral of any kind in their little life. The first being Grandma was a hard lump to swallow.

On July 5th, 2006 I left the girls sleeping at their aunt's house while I met my Aunt Barb at the Fort Collins Airport. Once again, bringing my mom's ashes along with me in the car, I made it to the airport for our morning flight to scatter my mom's ashes above the Buckhorn Canyon. It was a very beautiful morning. A little chill in the air, but a wonderful day for my mom to fly above the Rockies. Her spirit had been free for almost five months by now, but this would be her final wish. The pilot was kind enough to fly around just to the right area where I thought she would love to be. My hand pushed on the little lever as my Aunt and I began to cry. I could see the ashes being pulled from the container and trailing behind the small plane. That was it, there is nothing left of what was once my beautiful mom. Her hair was a beautiful blonde, her eyes were an amazing light blue, she had a wonderful smile and a brilliant mind. Those images of her will always be left in my memory.

The anniversary of her death came so quickly. The blink of an eye and time stops for no one. The past 12 months have been half in a trance and half semi-conscious. In that time our lives have been so much less chaotic. On February 15th, 2006 I dropped the girls off at school. I was sitting at a stop light on Cuyamaca Street thinking of my mom. It had been a year since she passed. I was thinking that I would email KYXY and ask them to play the song "Hero" for my mom. When the light turned green and I started to pull forward, I saw one white dove fly in front of my car. My dove; my mom.

As soon as I got home, I sent in my special email request to KYXY in San Diego. I told them about my mom, her passing, the sky changing and their radio station playing "Hero" immediately after I was speaking to her in the sky. The mid-morning DJ Sam Bass received my email and worked it out with his producer to play the song along with a special tribute for my mom. He emailed me back and forth over eight times letting me know when and how. He didn't know me from Adam, but the whole episode pulled at his heartstrings too.

At 1:00 p.m. Sam Bass spoke such wonderful words about my mom. He told of her life as a widowed mother of 5, how she started with nothing and was president of 5 banks in Colorado and owned one by the time she was 34. He mentioned the God-like rays of sunlight shining through a dismal day, and my daughter singing the song "Hero," as he began to play it for her once again. It was the most beautiful tribute I could have wished for. I sat at my computer crying for all of it, their kindness, my mom's death, life, sickness, happiness and sadness for missing her so much. I just wish that I could hug her again.

After the song was over, I called Sam to personally thank him. He was typing me a response email telling me he had several people who called in because it was such a touching story. One man was in the Marines and had just lost his mother a few months back. He was so touched he started to cry and had to hang up the phone. Even Sam had a choked-up voice when I spoke with him. Sam really made it apparent to me that people need to know there is more to our life when we die. There are messages, if we just slowed down enough to see them. We like to hear true stories that have miracles about our loved ones reaching out to us from beyond our physical life. It gives us a comfort and contentment in accepting death and where we go afterwards. Sam really gave me the idea to write this book and pull together more heartfelt stories like mine.

In the past few months I have been desperately searching the sky to take a picture of the God-clouds for the cover of this book. On April 21st 2006, my daughter Kalie was singing the National Anthem opening night at the Lakeside Rodeo. She was very nervous. It was her first performance in front of such a large crowd. I picked her and her sister Emily up early from school so we could get ready and eat. I pulled out a gold chain from a box of Grandma's personal effects. It was for Kalie from

Grandma. I called Kalie into my room and told her that this was a special gift from Grandma and that she wanted her to have it for a very special day. This day was the special day for her. I told her that Grandma would be there with her and not to be scared. She proudly hung the gold chain around her neck and gave me a big hug.

After dinner, my husband, the girls and I loaded up in his truck to head towards the rodeo. It was about 5:30 p.m. As we were pulling onto the main road towards Lakeside, the entire sky was filled with God-clouds. There they were! The ones that I had been trying to find for the past two months! The ray of light was shining through every direction of clouds in the sky and it was directly above the Lakeside Rodeo Grounds. I took photo after photo after photo. Kalie had the biggest message from Grandma too. Grandma had first-row seats up in the sky watching her 10-year-old granddaughter sing the world's most famous song. The message from the clouds that night made Kalie so happy, and she knew that her grandma was there cheering her on.

Just when I feel like I have written enough of my mom's little messages to me, I have but one last bittersweet message to add to my story. Today is May 20th, 2006. It has been just a few weeks past the two-year mark of my mom's initial diagnosis. On Monday May 15th, the trucking company called me at 1:00 to tell me that the driver was five minutes away with the Corvette.

I couldn't let that car go, so I bought it from my brother Ron. My intentions were to get it out here at the beginning of the year, but circumstances and finances always prevail. Now, on Mother's Day, my mom's Corvette is being delivered in all of its glory. The road to our house has a really tight corner so I told the driver to give me a few minutes to walk out to the main road to meet him so he didn't get stuck.

And then wouldn't you know it, the same radio station, the same Sam Bass, and my mom smiling down from heaven, as I hear Mariah Carey once again belt out "Hero." Thank you mom, I do hear you, and the Vetter is doing great! I'll take good care of your car and remember your smile while you would drive it!

I truly feel it in my heart that these signs are my mom. Those of you who can relate and have had your own experiences know what it means. No matter what anyone could possibly say to justify coincidence, or to believe themselves, I believe, and that is all that matters.

In Loving Memory of

Beverly Ann Mucha

February 16, 1945 - February 15, 2005

By: Julie A. Aydlott

Wayne

Wayne was my best friend ever. We did everything together, like skipping school, stealing our mom's canned peaches and sitting in the dog-house while eating them . . . We would watch the Wizard of Oz on TV and when it was over, we would go outside and pretend that we were the characters in the "Land of Oz." He was the best brother and friend you could ever ask for. He was very special because he had an ever-so-slight case of retardation, but you would never know it by the way he would draw, and from his music. We had a very special bond from day one, except of course when we would have our little fights as brothers and sisters do. Wayne was very protective of me because I was the baby of the family. He was always there for all of us. That was just the way he was.

Wayne had a lot of friends from the neighborhood as well as school. He had one really good friend named Terry. They were always hanging out together. Wayne and Terry's favorite place to hang out was around South Omaha, trying to pick up girls. Of course this was the late sixties when cool cars and girls went hand in hand. Terry would always come over to our house, and Wayne would play his guitar for him.

Wayne and Terry were out one night in May, and it was pretty late. I'm not sure where they were or where they were going, but Wayne was driving his car and Terry was in the passenger seat. Another car was coming towards them in the wrong lane. Wayne swerved to keep from hitting the other car, but ended up crashing into a large, round concrete railroad pillar. The impact was so strong that it pushed the engine into his lap and chest. The broken glass from the windshield was embedded into his eyes and brain.

About two o'clock in the morning the phone rang, and when my dad answered the phone, this voice on the other end said, "Hey, your son is dead." My dad didn't know who the caller was. Some time later we found out that the caller was the person who was driving the other car. They apparently recognized my brother's car, and from the severity of the accident and how long it took the firefighters to get him out, assumed that he couldn't have survived that accident, and was dead.

Not long after the first phone call, the police came to my house and told my parents that Wayne was taken to County Hospital. They said he was still alive but in very critical condition. My parents woke me up to tell me about the accident and told me to get dressed to go to the hospital. As I was frantically getting ready, my dad called my brother Bobby and told him what had happened. Everyone was crying and in a complete state of shock. We rushed to the hospital to see him, and when we got there, I saw him lying in the hospital bed. I couldn't believe that he looked like that. It was the hardest thing I ever had to face. His eyes were all cut up and swollen from the glass, his body crushed, and he just lay there without any movement.

I sat down next to my brother, talking to him and hoping he could hear me. I kept telling him to wake up even though I knew that would never happen. The doctors said that he wouldn't even make it through the night. Everyone was starting to arrive at the hospital, both of my older sisters Marilyn and Joanne, and my brother Bobby and his wife Beverly. The night turned into day, and when Wayne's girlfriend heard about the accident, she came to the hospital to see him too.

After two days of intensive care, Wayne passed away on May 24, 1968. He was only eighteen years old. I remember leaving the hospital with Wayne's girlfriend to get something to eat. While we were gone, the doctor had come out and told my parents that he was very sorry, "Your son didn't make it."

We went to the funeral home the day he was ready for viewing. I looked at him and couldn't stop crying. I thought to myself, "Now there he is, this looks like Wayne, only he looks as though he is sleeping." Even after his death we had a connection.

I was completely heartbroken. I lost my best friend and my brother. I don't remember helping to plan the funeral. I don't know if it was because I was only fifteen or because I was in a state of shock and disbelief. I do remember the funeral, though. The funeral home was filled beyond belief with flowers. They ran out of places to put them.

My older brother Bobby took it the hardest. Wayne was his baby brother and always looked up to Bobby. Before they closed the casket Bobby put some money in Wayne' pocket and said, "Here's some spending money for you." There were so many people at the funeral home that it was standing room only. On the way to the cemetery, the procession of cars was two miles long. You couldn't even see the end of the line. They had a hard time fitting all the cars in the parking area. We were so overwhelmed. We had never dreamed he had that many friends, but he did. I didn't want to say goodbye to Wayne, but it was time that I had to, knowing I would never see my sweet brother again.

After the funeral, we all went to Bobby's house. I was sitting in the living room looking out the "closed window" when there was a very strong smell of flowers. It was like I was in a florist shop, it was very strong. After a few minutes of smelling the flowers, it just went away, and I had a peace come over me, like he was telling me, "It's okay, I don't hurt anymore."

Wayne made another visit to us one night when it was really late. I was at Bobby's house again, and we were sitting at the kitchen table. Bobby's musical equipment was set up downstairs in the basement, where Wayne use to play with him a lot. Somehow, Bobby's guitar and amplifier turned on. We could hear music coming from the basement. Wayne loved to play the guitar and was very good at it. The music was very soft, almost as if he was afraid of waking everyone up. Bobby asked us if anyone had turned on his equipment and forgot to turn it off. None of us had even been downstairs. Bobby told us that everything was turned off when he originally went to bed. At that moment when we were all wondering how the music was coming from downstairs, all of a sudden we all could smell the incredible fragrance of the flowers again. His presence felt so strong, I knew at that moment that it was Wayne's way of letting me know that he was watching over us. Every time I would smell the strong scent of the flowers, I knew he was there.

The last time I sensed Wayne around was in 2005. I was going through a tough time with my husband, and I drove to the Bellevue Marina. I was going to drive into the river. I sat there for fifteen minutes, looking at the water, when I smelled the faint smell of flowers. I don't know what happened, but I somehow I got turned around and was driving back out of the Marina. I guess Wayne really wanted me to know he was there, and didn't want me to do anything so drastic. That's the last time I smelled the flowers. I can't prove it was him, but, I can't prove that it wasn't. All I know is when I smell the flowers, he is around.

In Loving Memory of

Wayne Mucha

July 18, 1949 – May 24, 1968

By: Patty Mucha-Rybin

Antonio

When I was a little girl, I had a special bond with my daddy. Many girls experience this same type of bond with their fathers. My daddy was a truck driver, so I had to hold my memories of him and used them to carry me through waiting for him to return home from his trips. It was that very thing, holding on to the memories, that helped me to remember him after he was gone.

Right around the time that I turned six years old, Daddy and my mother found out that he had leukemia. This was not something that was revealed to me or my siblings. I knew something was wrong, because he seemed a bit changed, but I was too young to vocalize my suspicions.

I remember very well the Christmas of 1981. It was perhaps the best Christmas I had ever had in my short life. My family wasn't wealthy, and in earlier years, we had to depend on charitable organizations just so we would have a Thanksgiving or a Christmas. This year in particular, I remember that I got almost everything that I dreamed of having, and then some. One thing I remember most about Christmas that year was my daddy's smile.

It was right after Christmas when it all went downhill. My brothers Tim and Mike were in my room with me. We were playing with our new Christmas toys. I remember hearing my mother crying, and there was a lot of yelling. I came out of my room in time to see my daddy in the bathroom. It wasn't good, and my mother slammed the door so that I wouldn't see what was happening. She had my brothers take me to my uncle's house so that I wouldn't see. We stayed at my uncle's house, and during this time, I couldn't stop crying. Things got worse when I heard the ambulance come for my daddy. My imagination was probably much worse than the reality. The thought that he might be scared was the worst part for me.

My daddy was taken to the hospital, where he would remain until he passed. During the time that he was in the hospital, my mother slept there, right alongside of him. Days would pass and I wouldn't see her. I became anxious, because I had this need to see my daddy, and soon. Instinctively, I knew that he was dying. I never got the chance to go to the hospital to see my daddy, and he passed away about a week into the New Year on January 6, 1982.

My whole world was just destroyed, and I felt so empty when I was told of his passing. Everything was such a blur. I couldn't really say for sure exactly who told me. I honestly don't remember my mother telling me of his death, because I think she was so overwhelmed. I do remember that I was at my uncle's house and that after I was told, my brother Anthony picked me up and held me for the longest time. I cried onto his shoulder for what seemed like an eternity before I finally just lay in his arms, completely limp.

The night that my daddy died, I stayed at my uncle's house. My mother, my brothers, and I were all cramped into my cousin's bedroom. We slept there together, drawing comfort from one another's presence. I remember lying there that night, crying as quietly as I could, just begging for God to please give my daddy back to me. I made many promises, figuring that if I just promised God that I would be good enough, he may let me have my daddy back.

Of course, those were the hopes and wishes of a child who had so much faith. I was lost in my own grief, and couldn't figure out how to "make it all better," since making it better was always my daddy's job. Some time during that night, my crying stopped. I don't know how, because I could have cried a river of tears. For some reason, I grew silent. As I lay there I felt a presence. I knew I wasn't alone, but I couldn't explain it. It felt comforting and safe. It felt like love. It felt like Daddy. I could smell his cologne in the room. I lost consciousness at that point, and slept all through the remainder of that night.

Months had passed, and my family was doing the best that we could in moving on with our lives. Everything I did, everywhere I went, I was reminded of my daddy. I would go to school, and I would remember him coming to my school to have lunch with me. I would see everything that I remembered so clearly in my mind's eye. At home, I would picture him as he always was, sitting at the kitchen table. To me, he wasn't gone at all, just out on another trip.

Several months after his passing, I was beginning to feel better. I wasn't crying every day anymore. Every night when I would go to bed, I would lie there and think about my day, and I would imagine wonderful things for myself and my life. It was my way to wind down, and dream of my future. Whenever I admitted to myself the reality, that my daddy wouldn't BE in my future, I would feel sad.

The first night that he appeared to me, I was still awake, lying in my bed. As little girls often do, I had been imagining my wedding day. I imagined everything, down to the last detail, the dress I would wear and what my husband would look like. Then, I began thinking that my daddy wouldn't be there to give me away. I told myself that I was not going to cry, and I reminded myself of what my mother had told me, that Daddy wouldn't want me to be sad.

Then, slowly, I began to see this faint light next to my bed. It was white and dim. It started about halfway off of the floor and grew from the center outward. I sat up in bed because I didn't know what it was. I wasn't afraid. I didn't feel that I should be. Then, inside the light, I saw my daddy. He was smiling and was just as handsome as I had ever remembered seeing him. He didn't say anything; he just reached his hand out to me. Then, he faded, but I still felt as if he was there. I felt comforted. I fell asleep and wasn't aware of anything else until I woke up the next morning.

Several nights passed, and I didn't see Daddy. I began to think that I had been dreaming, but I kept telling myself that I knew that I was not dreaming, because I was very aware of everything around me. Then, he appeared again. This time, there wasn't much light, and he appeared simultaneously with the light. He was sitting on the edge of my bed, and was smiling down at me. I lay there and just began talking to him. I told him about my day, and how much I'd missed him. He sat there, as he had in life, and I actually felt him stroking my hair. Even at the tender age of six years, I knew then that he was always with me, no matter what.

His visits were irregular, in that there was no set pattern. He didn't come to me every night, and I didn't question why. I was just glad that he was there at all. Evidently, he wasn't coming to me every night because he was visiting the rest of my family as well.

The first thing I remember that could have been attributed to Daddy's visits, was when my mother told us that she was getting a new bed in which to sleep. She said that she couldn't stand sleeping in that bed without my daddy actually being there, and that she felt him there, when she knew he was not. She thought he wasn't, but I believe that he was.

My mother started talking about our home in general, and said it was filled with too many memories. She said that everywhere she turned, he was there. I know she wasn't frightened; but more likely, she needed him to be with us in the physical sense, and was frustrated that although she could feel him, he wasn't there in body. She told me in later years that she would stand in the kitchen while cooking dinner, and hear him talk to her over her shoulder. He would even correct her if she was preparing something differently than he did when he was alive.

My daddy was quite active for a time in the home. During this time, a close family friend was visiting. Everyone had left the house except for her, and she decided to do dishes before she joined us. She said that while she stood at the kitchen sink, she felt a chill in the air, and felt goose bumps rising on her arms. Then, she felt someone touch her on the shoulder. She did become uneasy, and at the time, it didn't cross her mind that it could have been Daddy. She left the house and went to join us at my uncle Earl's home, because she couldn't explain who had touched her.

When I found out about this, I knew that it couldn't be anyone but my daddy. I suppose that things began to be too much for my mother. I know that he wasn't attempting to frighten anyone. He was more or less trying to communicate and offer comfort to those who loved him. Perhaps my mother just needed a fresh start. Nevertheless, my mother made the decision to move from that home into a new one.

After moving into our new home, I didn't see my daddy anymore, at least not during my childhood. I felt sad, and missed him even more. I became depressed, and began having health problems. I got physically ill quite regularly, which was attributed to the stress of losing him.

The years passed, and as I grew up, I began to think that I had imagined my father's visits. I even told myself that it was a subconscious coping strategy that caused me to see him. Occasionally I would dream of him, and in the dreams, he was always unattainable. I would try to get to him, and he would disappear, or be walking away, and wasn't able to hear me call out to him. This proved to be stressful for me, as well. I took these dreams as nothing but dreams, or more like nightmares, since I couldn't reach him. I began to try to control my dreams, so that I would have the chance to hug him once more . . . if not in reality, at least in my dreams.

Life for my family moved on. My mother began to date again and started to resemble herself again. She had been equally depressed, and understandably so. It's hard to lose a parent, and I know that pain, but I have not felt the pain of losing a companion, the person with whom you plan to spend the rest of your life. I can only imagine what she went through during the grieving process. She dated, but not seriously, because she hadn't felt she'd found the right one.

My brothers and I grew and matured. We had pulled ourselves up, and had begun doing well again in school. We were finally adjusting. My mother eventually did meet a wonderful man, and they married when I was twelve years old. I couldn't imagine a better stepfather, and I believe that in some way, my daddy watched over us, even if I didn't feel him, until my mother found the right person who would protect us and care for us.

The years passed, and I was a teenager. I was not as rebellious as some teens are, and in many ways, I was more mature than my peers, because I had been through things that some had not. I had started a tradition when I was a child. I would always talk to Daddy after I said my prayers. This is a tradition that I continue with, even to this day. I never saw Daddy, but I would feel him sometimes when I would talk to him. I just felt that he could hear me.

I began to become a bit more daring, and even though I had adjusted, I would have bouts of depression. During one of these periods, I began to think about suicide. It was a dumb idea, to entertain such a thing, but in my mind, I thought that if I committed suicide, I would be able to be with my daddy again. Not a whole lot makes sense when you are depressed and have thoughts as I have described. I told no one, but I began to plan my demise. I actually sat, prepared to follow through with my plans, when I heard my daddy's voice in my ear. He told me that he didn't raise me to be weak like that, and that he wouldn't want me to end my life in such a manner. Then, he told me to think of my mother, and how much she would be hurt.

I stopped right where I was, and I listened. I knew he was right. I yelled out to him, asking him where he'd been and why he hadn't been there for me. I was answered with silence. I knew then that I could not take my life, but I became angry with him. I wanted to know why he hadn't been there for me before this. I didn't get an answer that day, but I did, eventually get my answer.

The day of my high school graduation in June of 1993 was very eventful. A storm had suddenly rolled in while I was on my way to a friend's home before we were to be graduated. I made it safely to her home, but the electrical storm was quite intense, and I was too frightened to get out of the car. The heavy downpour wasn't letting up, and my car was parked beneath a tree. Now I was frightened that lightning might strike the tree and hit my car. As I sat there, lightning struck just behind my car. I didn't know what to do, but my fear made me jump out of the car and run for the safety of my friend's home. As I was running up the steps, lightning struck right beside me. I continued to run up the steps and into my friend's home. I knew I was lucky, but I also knew that my daddy was with me.

After the storm had passed, my friend and I drove to the graduation ceremony. There were trees down everywhere, and lots of damage. Our outdoors graduation was ruined, and we had to have the ceremony indoors in the gym of the school. I was quite emotional, and I kept thinking of Daddy. During the whole ceremony, I felt him as if he were right beside me. I was shedding tears over the ending of one part of my life, the beginning of the next part, the trauma that had occurred earlier, and from the relief that my daddy was there for me. It's a moment I will never forget.

After graduating high school, I moved to another city and began a new chapter in my life. I was at the time of life when you are anticipating what your future holds, and discovering that you are now an adult. I lived life to the fullest, and had fun with my friends. It was my first taste of real freedom, and I loved it. During this period, I didn't feel my daddy anywhere. I continued to talk to him, though.

I eventually met my husband, and fell totally in love. When we were to be married, my daddy was ever-present in my mind. I didn't have any sense that he was with me at the wedding, and was rather disappointed. I just knew that he would be there when it really counted. My wedding was simple, but beautiful. I was so very happy on my wedding day, despite missing my daddy.

My first year of marriage passed rather quickly, and my daughter Meghan was born. My husband and I were so proud. The day I gave birth, I somehow thought that I would feel my daddy with me. I didn't feel him, but my happiness over having my first child was so great, that I wasn't upset or disappointed. I just knew in my heart that if there were a way for Daddy to be there, he would be, and I had faith in that thought.

When my daughter was five months old, my husband and I got an unexpected surprise: we were going to have another baby. I was a bit scared of the idea, since I was anxious over having more than one baby at a time, but my fear turned into joy. About a month after I found out about the pregnancy, I fell ill, and had a high fever. For days, I was so sick that I couldn't hold my head up. My main concern was my daughter, because she had gotten ill, as well. However, I had a bad feeling about the baby that I was carrying. I knew my temperature was too high, and I worried about the baby that was growing inside of me. My fears were confirmed when I went to visit my doctor and found that I was miscarrying.

I lost the baby, and was devastated. I named the baby, so that I could properly grieve. For the baby that I would never get to hold, I chose the name of an angel: Gabriel. The depression of my youth came back with full force, and I don't remember ever having a darker time in my life, before or since. For months, I could do nothing but cry. I couldn't pull myself out of it, and the medications that my doctors prescribed did little to help. I was miserable and cried myself to sleep nightly.

One night, I was so overwhelmed with grief and depression. I prayed, and then began speaking to my daddy. I don't know how long I talked to him before I finally fell asleep. Then, I began to dream. At first, the dreams were nonsense, just bits and pieces of dream that didn't really fit together. Then, a miracle happened.

Suddenly, I was face to face with my daddy. He stood before me, just as handsome as I remembered him. He had a look of concern, and I noticed the softness of his brown eyes. I began crying, and telling him how much I missed him. I started to tell him about all that had happened, and he stopped me. He told me that he knew everything. He told me that even though I hadn't felt him, he had heard me every time I talked to him. A tear came to his eye, and he said that he knew about my baby, and he knew the hurt that I was feeling.

I asked him where he'd been, and he told me that he had been there all the time. I wanted to know why I didn't feel him. He told me that he didn't know, but he did know that I felt him when it counted the most. He went on to tell me that my daughter was beautiful, and that she looked just like I did when I was a baby. He said that he had been there for her birth. He also said that he had been there when I was married. He told me I was beautiful then and even though there was no way he could walk me down the aisle to give me away, he stood beside me during the whole ceremony.

I began to cry harder, and he hugged me. That was the one thing that I had missed and wanted more than anything: to feel him hug me one more time. He wiped my tears, as he had done many times when I was a little girl. Then, he grabbed my arms and told me that he wanted me to listen to him.

I stood there, and he told me that he knew how hard it was for me to lose my baby. He said that even though it seemed unfair, my baby wasn't allowed to be born, because I wasn't ready for him just yet. He went on to tell me that I needed to be getting ready for something very special.

He told me that I was going to have a son soon, and that he was destined for great things. He told me to hold fast to that knowledge and to concentrate all my efforts on my daughter, and that she and my husband needed me. He didn't want me to dwell on the baby I lost, but to concentrate on the one that I already had, and the son that was to come. Then, he said he had to go, but for me to know that he was always with me, and told me to look for signs from him from time to time.

When I awoke the next morning, I felt changed. For the first time in months, I had hope, and was actually able to bring a smile to my face. I concentrated on my daughter and my husband, just as my daddy had told me to do. The dream of him had helped me to move toward healing.

I told my husband the morning following my dream, of what my daddy had told me. He was a bit surprised, but he said that he believed that when we lose someone, it is very possible for them to come to us in dreams, when we are most open.

Two weeks after I had my dream, I realized that I needed to take a pregnancy test. When I took it, it immediately came back positive. I was elated, and I just knew that I was going to have a boy! I was a bit scared, because I was afraid of losing this baby, as well, but I held fast to what my daddy had told me, and had faith that everything would be okay. My pregnancy was a happy and healthy one, with no complications. I felt truly blessed, and anxious to meet my new son!

When I gave birth to my son Steven, on May 17, 2001, I had my cousin and my husband with me.

I was glad to have my family and husband there. I didn't feel my father, but I knew, since my dream, that he was there, watching over me and my baby. The delivery was an easy one, compared to other stories I have heard. As soon as the doctor announced that it was a boy, I smiled and whispered to my daddy, a quiet thank you. My cousin commented on how much my son looked like my daddy.

Ever since the birth of my son, I haven't felt, seen, nor dreamed of my father, but I have watched for the signs that he said would tell me he was there. I think he uses coins to let me know he is around. Not long after my youngest son Chandler was born, I was able to enjoy a rare moment to sleep in. My husband was caring for the baby, since I wasn't getting enough rest.

I got up that morning, and went to the bathroom. While I was at the sink, I felt something come from nowhere and hit my leg from the side. I heard it hit the floor after hitting my leg, and when I looked down, I saw that it was a penny. I didn't think anything of it, and assumed it must have been on the counter and I just hadn't noticed it before.

I decided to go back to bed to catch a bit more sleep before I started my day. When I went back to my bed, I laid down and felt something cold. When I lifted the covers, I saw a stack of quarters, which had been tipped over when I got in bed, and were now spread out. I knew that they had not been there before I went to the bathroom, because it was where I had just been lying down. They would have still been warm. When I picked up the quarters, each and every one of them was cold, and each and every one of them were state quarters. The state that was represented on every one of the quarters was Rhode Island. Rhode Island was where my father was born. I knew beyond a shadow of a doubt, that my father was letting me know that he was there.

Since then, I have only been able to get the signs that he is around. Usually I will find coins in places where there weren't any before. I've had one instance where I got into my car, and found a Rhode Island state quarter in the driver's seat. At various times I've had coins come from out of nowhere to smack me on the arm or leg. I usually get "hit" with the coins when I am feeling down or stressed. He also comes in other forms. The first Christmas after my daddy died, my mother bought a Christmas bell which plays music. It adorned our tree every year, and when I was out on my own, my mother entrusted it to me. Occasionally, the bell will start playing music on its own. When it happens, I just smile, and say, "Hi Daddy."

In Loving Memory of

Antonio Garcia

May 27, 1930 – January 6, 1982

By: Laura Garcia Reed

Les

One week before my dad passed away, he and I joked about him being grumpy. He could only gargle when he tried to speak, as he was still adjusting to the new tracheotomy. I would place my ear near his mouth, but his words were unclear. I simply communicated through his piercing blue eyes, and his hand gestures would also help me understand what he was trying to convey. He was alert and lucid, but probably had lost count of how many hospital transfers he had; and that night was another. If I had known then that in four days he would be immobile and three days later, I would never see those baby blues again, I would have visited a little longer.

Four days later was unbearable. His flesh, or of what was left of him, was cold to the touch. I gave him a foot massage and with his eyes closed and mouth open, he could only respond with a slight grin to let me know that he could feel the warmth on to the soles of his feet. Three days later, he was comatose. I held his hand for six hours knowing that the end was near. I didn't want him to be alone when he would take his last breath.

A lot of thoughts went through my mind, but mostly I felt guilty that he was in this predicament. Countless doctors and numerous transfers, I lost track after a while, but will always remember the pungent odor that lingered on his body. If I smell it again in my lifetime, I'll know that it is cancer and death is imminent. As I held his hand and lay my head on his bedside, I felt a presence over my right shoulder. I looked up to see if any nurse had come in, but no nurse ever came in during my last visit. The last thing I had heard from the nurse was that Dad was in euphoria and time was of the essence.

I must have looked over my shoulder a dozen times and stared where the IV pole stood. The presence was tall and broad and it made itself known by leaving a scuff mark on my chin. I don't know how to explain the scuff mark. I occasionally get them on my body for unknown reasons. It's almost like a hickey, but smaller. The presence that I felt was definitely a male figure; perhaps it was his father, my grandpa, guarding his son, waiting patiently to guide Dad on to the other side.

I had a hard time leaving that day, but after six hours and with a two-hour drive home, I knew I had to go. My heart wanted to hold him until the end, but physically I had to get going. It took me a while to leave, as I would pace back and forth from the hallway back into his room. I wanted to make sure he was okay before I left for the last time. I quietly said my good-bye and walked out of the hospice.

Eleven p.m. January 26, 2006, time of death, is noted on his death certificate, but I think he left this world a few hours earlier and it was only discovered at that time when the new shift began. I feel terrible that he was in that cold, dark room all by himself, but I should have known that it would be his style to perform the last act in solitude.

The days after were a blur, but I knew I had to prepare for the memorial. My aunt Kate, Dad's only sister, had contacted me to go to the funeral home. She and I were the primary caretakers since Dad's hospitalization. I have to admit that I was avoiding her messages. I just wanted to curl up in bed and not come out for couple of days. I was exhausted and she was too. She confided in me that she felt relieved after he passed away. I didn't share her same comfort. In fact, I felt that I had failed him. I often think if I had spent more time or that if I had done something different, he would have been stronger. Avoiding my aunt's calls was futile. I finally spoke to her and she directed me to go to the funeral home to sign papers as the power of attorney. She must have heard or felt my resistance for what I had to do, so she accompanied me. I sat at the table at the funeral home with tunnel vision and signed page after page of unread documents. All I could focus on with each page was the name of the deceased. By the fifth page of signing, an overwhelming feeling came over me; it was like a ton of bricks to acknowledge that my dad was dead, and I stopped signing. I put the pen down and began to bawl. "I can't do this," I told my aunt. She held my hand and told me that it was okay to take my time. I composed myself and finished signing, but I was miserable knowing that I had signed his life away and it was the ultimate good-bye.

Dad, on the other hand, was not ready to say his good-byes. Signs began to appear not long after the memorial. The first sign was a dove. This particular dove had grayish-blue wings and it mysteriously began hanging around the house. I knew this dove was a sign from my dad, as it had never been seen before, and it was extremely unusual to see a dove in the dead of winter. This dove would perch on the roof as if he was guarding the house. I interpreted the dove perching as a sign of protection. Not only was he watching over me, but my whole family.

I remember vividly one morning as my heart ached of Dad's passing, when I stepped outside and the dove flew right over my head. It came so close that my hair flung in the air. It gave me a calming sensation that he is always there when I think of him. The dove sighting diminished after about two weeks. I have yet to see another gray-blue dove since.

The next sign from my dad was when the wind chime would sway by itself. It took me a while to notice that it would swing without a hint of wind. Sound of pipes clanging softly makes music like angels on harps. Every time I hear the music, I look up in the trees to see if the leaves are moving, and often they are not. I simply smile and secretly say, "Hi Dad" under my breath.

The most significant sign for me occurred one day when my family got together. It was a day of cleaning Dad's storage and the family had planned to meet for lunch before we were to sort his treasures. It was strange that I had worn a denim jacket that day which I had not worn in years. I sat next to my niece who oddly enough was wearing a denim jacket as well, and we began comparing our pockets. I placed my hand in the outer pocket of my left breast over my heart. I felt something in the pocket, and whatever it was, I was determined to find out. I could only scrape off pieces of lint so then I decided to take the jacket off, reversed the pocket and was able to pull out a wad of previously washed and dried paper, now almost like clay. I could have simply thrown it away, but I kept peeling at it, a little piece at a time, as I was trying to figure out if it had been a phone number or a receipt for something. I don't know why, but I wouldn't give up until a piece peeled off with the letters "les." The letters spell my dad's name. I knew it was a sign from him saying that he was there among us.

After lunch, we proceeded to go to the storage. The storage was long and narrow, twenty feet by four feet. He had couple of tool boxes, an old brief case, and boxes of what I call junk. None of us had a plan, but our goal was to empty the storage. My sisters began going through his things to keep whatever they wanted for themselves. I began carrying things out of the storage and lined them up along the outside wall. Dad was known as a meticulous character. It was nice to see things still intact, unwrapped, or unscratched that I hadn't seen since childhood. I felt his presence there. Dad was definitely there, breathing down our necks. He was ordering us to be careful with a particular box, or not to throw away his pipes, is what I heard subconsciously. We spent hours there for the small amount he had. Maybe it was our way of showing our emotions to the person, as even though he was not a major part of our lives, we felt compelled to not depart from him so quickly. We threw away very little, and each of our cars was full. My mom, his ex-wife, decided to come home with us, and that's where the next sign appeared.

It was an ordinary Friday in March and I had picked up my daughters. Making dinner and bath for my toddler was the normal routine. It was not until bedtime for my toddler that she had her first sighting of Dad. The light had been dimmed and I was lying on her bed with her. I was humming a sweet melody for her to fall asleep. She calmly pointed at the wall at the end of her feet and said, "Gran-pa."

I saw nothing but a blank wall. It startled me that she could see him. I immediately got goose bumps, but didn't let her know that I was scared. I comforted her and told her that "Gran-pa" was just watching over us. I have no doubt in my mind that she saw him that night. She has shown clairvoyance since infancy and I had to expect it. I didn't stay in her room too long, I have to admit, as I was little freaked out.

I came out of the room and told my husband and mom what had happened, but they didn't believe me. My mom was too involved in reading the letters that she had seized from the storage. I was not aware that she had found letters dating back to before I was born. The letters were correspondences from my dad to his own mother during the time that he was married to my mom and living abroad. There was ten years worth of air-grams.

I started reading the letters that Mom had already finished. The years dated on the letters were sporadic so I decided to put them in chronological order to have a better understanding of his life. Reading the letters was like a short movie in fast forward. Vivid memories appeared and facts unknown to me were disclosed. I was anxious to read the part that would reveal why Dad left the family, but it was never mentioned, or if it was, I must have skimmed through it. It didn't matter anymore as I had forgiven him a long time ago. The way he articulated his day-to-day living was captivating. I was up past midnight reading those letters.

One of the memorable letters was the announcement of another baby due. I could feel his hopefulness that the last child might be of a different sex, but unfortunately, I was born a girl like all of the others. His letters were honest and shed his true feelings. They were written in a way that answered his mother's questions from the previous correspondence, so that it was almost like listening to them talk. He confided in his mother with his deepest secrets. One letter was heartbreaking to me; he was despondent with his life's failures. He wrote about his disheartening days during military service and his hardship during college that resulted in giving up his first-born. His words continued to dismay me, with the sorrow of his simple wedding day that took place at the embassy, when he expressed with such sadness how he had to place his new bride on a train home alone.

Mom later told me that she fell asleep crying from the hurtful words in those letters. Mom, I know, has a heart of a stone and a strong will, and expressing emotions are her cultural taboo. I have never seen her shed tears until Dad's passing. I felt bad for her that she had to relive the truth through written words. Maybe Dad was remorseful and was there to comfort her that night. My mom left the following morning to stay with my sister Jill. My toddler Ella never spoke of a vision in that house again.

The next sign from Dad wouldn't come until the summer. It was my niece's birthday party and I knew that Ella would fall asleep during the long drive to my sister's house. When we finally arrived, I had to fix Ella's hair before we could present ourselves. I reached to the back seat and unbuckled her car seat. I had asked her to come up front to fix her hair. I was busy looking for matching rubber bands and didn't notice Ella being fixated with something outside. She continued to stare without blinking and told me that she was scared. I asked her what she was scared of and her response was, "Gran-pa."

I had to smile at that moment, as it had been a while since she had spoken of him. I was not frightened by her remark; I simply asked her if she saw him and she nodded yes. I asked her where, but she did not point this time. I followed her eyes, but all I saw was that she was staring at an opened garage door at my sister's next door neighbor's house. I comforted her and told her to wave hello to him. She lifted her hand and waved with uncertainty.

I was curious as to what she was seeing and asked her simple questions. She said that "Gran-pa" did not have long hair and was scary looking. Dad's hair was shaven while hospitalized. He also had lost thirty pounds, to say the least. His cheeks became indented and were almost skeletal. That sight would make anybody look scary. I pondered my daughter's response and concluded that the spirit of the afterlife maintains its last known physical appearance, and that Dad would only appear near Mom.

Mom greeted us at the door and I told her and few guests what had just happened, but they just shrugged it off. I asked Mom by the outside garden if she felt his presence, but she said no. At the moment, I saw the most beautiful and biggest butterfly I have ever seen. It was about three inches in width and had sparkling black spots on bright orange wings. I pointed at it for Mom to see, but she was too occupied with the guests. I believe the butterfly was a sign of Dad that only I could see, because no one else made a comment on how pretty it was.

Now, six months later, I was excited to hear that Mom was coming to visit our new house. I was anxious to see if my daughter, now three years old, would detect Dad around Mom. Mom's visit was short and my daughter never mentioned anything about her gran-pa during her visit. I must confess that I was a little disappointed that my daughter no longer sees visions. I guess she has outgrown it, as I have read many young children do.

Next month will mark Dad's one-year departure from this physical world, but my family continues to encounter his spirits to this day. The extraordinary thing about Dad's spirit is that he appears among the living, within total strangers. Most recently was just last week when I saw him at a local coffee shop, sitting outside, alone. I was too frightened to go near him, as I did not want to exchange eye contact. I did not want to experience the fear as I did with the first stranger who possessed Dad. It occurred when my friend and I took a stroll at lunch time and a block up the street, where I could see a man disoriented and upset. He was yelling and throwing small rocks at a business window. As we approached him, I kept my distance and disregarded him. I try to avoid situations like that, but the man and I made eye contact, and the similarity of the piercing blue eyes was too coincidental. It frightens me to know that Dad's spirits are alive among the living.

One day, my husband frantically called me from a local department store and said that he had just passed my dad in an aisle and the man stared at him with his familiar blue eyes. His voice quivered, not from fear, but with excitement, as he has never experienced anything out of the ordinary. My husband Frank is the king of all skeptics. He has an engineering background that defines everything by logic and science. He has, however, become open-minded about the unexplained occurrences that he has encountered. It is he who first recognized the dove sightings, and with this latest bypass of a familiar stranger he has become definitely more intuitive.

My older daughter Mariah had an event occur when she was at a Chinese restaurant with her dad. She noticed a patron come in that looked a lot like her grandpa. She didn't think anything of it until she read her fortune cookie that said, "Remember the memories." Mariah said that her neck turned toward the elderly gentleman to follow his every step and that she doesn't recall the conversation taking place at the table with her dad. She said that she was awestruck by the message in the fortune cookie.

Mariah and I had an incident recently while shopping at a grocery store. The man in front of us at the check out line resembled Dad. I didn't share my thoughts with Mariah until she whispered,

"Mom, he looks like Grandpa," and I just grinned and agreed.

Dad's spirit lives on and it appears in many forms and shapes. I feel him and he lets me know he's thinking of me too when the wind chime sways.

In Loving Memory of

Les J. Coulter

August 18, 1934 – January 26, 2006

By: Annie Serda-Chavez

John "Vin"

My dad was my friend, and my hero. He was a gentle man with a kind heart who could touch the very core of your soul with his smile. Daddy was born in Limerick, Ireland on August 13, 1925 and was one of thirteen brothers and sisters. He came to the United States when he was a young man, bringing with him great stories of Irish lore and legend, which held us spellbound as children.

Daddy was a man of great faith. He believed in God and he prayed daily. When I was a young girl he worked as a printer; his hours were varied and included many evening shifts. I can remember no matter how tired he was when he arrived home, he would go to his bedroom with his prayer book and pray. Sunday mass was always a priority. His religion was a great part of who he was.

He was a simple man. Daddy never was one to need much. He would always say that as long as he had his family, he had everything in the world.

We knew we were cherished by him and he in turn was cherished by us.

Daddy found out quite by accident that he had lung cancer at the age of 76. He had gone to the doctor for a simple procedure, and a chest x-ray was given as part of the routine. I will never forget that cold January day I received the news. It was as if someone had taken all the air out of the room and I was slowly suffocating. I felt as if my world would never be the same again. Daddy took the news in stride. He refused to believe that he wouldn't beat this cancer, as he truly felt quite good. I turned all my energies toward research. I found out all there was to know about this disease and I prided myself on being able to be his advocate with his doctors. Daddy had chemo for three months and then God blessed him with two years of being "stable." His life didn't miss a beat. He continued golfing and being my mom's "bestest" buddy. They were quite a team and were never ever far from each other's side. As much as I worried about him, I was also consumed with worry for her, as I knew eventually she would be left without him.

It was springtime of 2004 and Daddy slowly started his decline. His battle became harder and harder and he knew his time with us was coming to an end. We had many, many long talks through the years about death and heaven. I vividly remember one afternoon in his hospital room, Daddy had just received more news about the cancer spreading further, and it was the first time he looked at me and said, "Sharon, I guess I am going to die." I was devastated and I held his hand and sobbed. I asked him if he was afraid. He looked up into my eyes and was almost insulted that I would ask that. "Am I afraid of dying?" he said. "No, of course not, I am going to a better place, I know that. What I am afraid of is saying goodbye to my family. I will miss you all very much." Daddy also made me a promise that day. He said, "If there is any way I can let you know I am okay and I made it to heaven, I promise you I will." I held onto that promise, and I reminded him numerous times through his final months that I would be waiting for that "sign" from him.

Spring turned to fall, and on a beautiful moonlit night, December 14, 2004, Daddy left this earth. I was on my way back to the hospital when I looked at the clock on the dashboard. It was 7:15 p.m. I knew immediately that Daddy was gone. A few minutes later, the cell phone rang and my sister, Doreen told me that our Dad had passed. We continued our journey back to the hospital and sat with Daddy. The whole family was there. We talked of all the good times and Mom just continued to stroke his hair and kiss him. It was so very painful for her to have to say goodbye to the man that was her life for 52 years. I stepped outside to the nurse's station and asked if they could tell me the exact time of my dad's death. The nurse shuffled through some paperwork and said what I already knew, "7:15 p.m."

On our ride home that night, I made a cell phone call to my office. As I was speaking, my cell phone "beeped" to let me know I had another call trying to get through. I chose to ignore the incoming phone call. A few minutes after I hung up the phone, I decided that I should check my missed calls list to see who was trying to reach me, and that's when it happened. There on the phone's display was one very simple message: **Missed It, Dad.**

I cried at first and then I began smiling and the most peaceful feeling entered my entire being. That gentle man with the kind heart had touched my soul again, only this time, it was indeed from heaven.

During the first few weeks after Daddy's passing, I would beg him to come and "visit" me, to give me another sign. I watched and waited. During this time my dog, Tucker, began acting strangely. He no longer would eat food from his dish, and he seemed "bothered" by something that I couldn't see. He would move cautiously from room to room acting skittish and somewhat nervous. There were times I would call him to come to me and he would walk around something to get to me, something that I could not see. I thought little of it, but this strange behavior continued on for weeks.

One evening a few months later, I went with a group of friends to someone who claimed to be able to "contact those on the other side." During her session, she turned to me and said, "You have the dog with the T name?" When I said "yes," she began smiling and said, "Your dad has been to visit you many times, but he says your poor dog is afraid, because your dad brings **his** dog along with him when he comes to see you." My dad indeed had a favorite dog who had passed before him. Daddy always wished to meet up with her again in heaven, and it makes me happy to know his wish was granted.

I feel so blessed to have received such strong signs from my dad, although I am not at all surprised by them. Daddy always put his family first while he was here with us, and he continues to let us know we still have a very special place in his heart. These are his final gifts to me, gifts that will be cherished forever.

In Loving Memory of

John Vincent Brosnahan

August 13, 1925 – December 14, 2004

By: Sharon Rutledge

Audrey

My mother was a very special role model for me and for my two daughters Amy and Megan. They were her only grandchildren and they called her "Granny." The four of us went everywhere together and did a lot of special things with each other. She was diagnosed with "Non small cell lung cancer stage 3B" on January 1st, 2006 and we were there with her for the entire fight. My youngest daughter Megan, who is 20, and I never missed a chemo or the thirty-three radiation appointments with her, so we talked a lot about different things in life. We talked a lot about the afterlife and what it would be like. My mom said that if she went first she would be my guardian angel. She would try and show us she is around in ways that we would know her. I joked with her about being a cardinal in my backyard and she agreed that of course she would be. We all believed that one day we would all be together again, hoping that of course the day we parted would not be for a long time yet.

My mom passed away on June 1st, 2006 after being in the hospital for three weeks. No one had expected for her to pass. She had her appointments set up for the next chemo session and the doctors kept saying that "you get to go home in a couple of days." But God has a way of taking control. She was only on hospice those last two days.

My mom had a sister named Karen that she was very close to. My aunt Karen could not be with her during this time, but she would call quite frequently to check on her. Right when Mom took her last breath at 7:08 p.m., my cell phone rang and it was Karen. The hospital room was packed with loved ones, and of course I was rubbing Mom's hair and couldn't get to my phone. Karen was determined to find out what was going on, and she called my uncle's cell phone. He was also in the room with us. My uncle answered his phone and told Aunt Karen that Mom had just passed at the exact same time she had called me. Karen was shocked, but completely believes that my mom was telling her good-bye.

We had a celebration of her life, no visitation, as she was cremated. It was just a gathering of friends and family at the funeral home. It was held on a beautiful June day, very sunny and with very little wind. Amy, Megan, Karen and I each gave a eulogy and talked about how wonderful she was. We had brought a CD to the funeral home that Mom had cherished. It was Vince Gill, and we asked the funeral director to play "Go Rest High on the Mountain." Mom loved this song, and it had been sung at her Mom's funeral five and a half years ago. Karen was the last to speak and when she sat down, the song came on and it was the wrong song. The funeral director tried several different tracks and none of them were right. It was the wrong CD. He made the announcement to the crowd of at least a hundred people that this had never happened to him in all of his years of doing this. I am sure Mom was saying, "This is a celebration, not a sad time."

After the celebration, we all went out back of the funeral home and we said a prayer and released sixty four balloons, one for each year of her life. We then released four white doves to symbolize her going to heaven. The two people who brought the doves released the first one, which represented Mom and was supposed to take off first. Well, she didn't; she sat in a tree and waited for the other three to be released, as she didn't want to go by herself. Once again, this had never happened to them.

The first four months after my mom passed were an absolute nightmare. One day in late September I had a horrible day at work, and I just wanted to talk to her. I was feeling sorry for myself walking out to my car. I got in and started the car and the radio was playing the song that was supposed to have been sung at her celebration, "Go rest high on the mountain" by Vince Gill. I started crying because I knew she was with me and telling me that it would be all right.

One of my mom's favorite things about my house was in my backyard, where there are a lot of birds. She loves birds, and her favorite bird is a cardinal. One day I wanted to have a cup of coffee with her as I did every day after work when she was alive, and now I couldn't. I was sitting at my kitchen table having my cup of coffee and meditating and thinking about "Mom," when I looked out my window and there were the reddest six cardinals I have ever seen in my life. Now when we see them out there we say "Granny is here."

As far back as I can remember my mom collected pennies. I'm not sure why, except she thought someday there would be a shortage. Now when my girls and I are doing something that "Granny" would enjoy, we will find a penny. It is like she is telling us, "Hey don't forget about me." We always pick the penny up, and say, "Granny, you are with us."

My stepdad Charlie would always tell jokes, and my mom would always respond with, "Heck of a deal." A lot of the family stayed in her room the night before she passed, and she was not responding for quite some time. It was in the middle of the night, and Charlie told a joke. Mom said as plain as day, "Heck of a deal" and laughed. We knew then that she would be with us forever. Those were her last words.

In Loving Memory of

Audrey Snow

January 26, 1942– June 1, 2006

By: Connie Lees

Johnny

"Love of a lifetime and beyond"

I was just turning fifteen when Johnny and I met in 1959. He was eleven years older than I. From the first moment that we met, there was something very special between us. Years later, we were to agree that there never seemed to be a time when we fell in love. We had loved forever and only had to meet.

Soon Johnny become like another member of my family. My mom loved him like another son, and he became best friends with one of my brothers. When I met his sister, the four of us would spend every minute together that we could.

Johnny was not only very handsome, but very talented as well. He had a guitar and a voice, and he knew how to use them. He had a way of putting all of the pain and joy of his life into his songs. Not long after we met, Johnny wrote a song for me. When I heard it, I was upset because I thought he had written it for someone else. He told me that the song was written for me. Our age difference gave him the idea for the song. One of the lines said, "They say I'm robbing the cradle, but I love you just the same."

Johnny and I had been seeing each other every day for several months when he just disappeared. My family searched for him for days, but he was nowhere to be found. We eventually had to admit that he was gone. I'm not quite sure what happened to me over the next few months. Somehow, despite having such a good memory, those days are lost to me. I imagine it was the pain from a broken heart.

I learned the real reason why Johnny disappeared forty years later. At this time in my life, I didn't know that one of my uncles had met him in the yard the last time Johnny came to see me. My uncle threatened to send him to jail because I was under 18. He told Johnny to get lost, and Johnny, not knowing my uncle had no say in my life, took him seriously. It was too hard for Johnny to stay and not be able to see me, so he caught a bus out of town that same night. Over a year after Johnny had left, I eventually met someone else. As I was planning our wedding and a new life, I found out that Johnny had come back to town. Because he was still friends with my brother, I saw him several times but never had the courage to ask the questions that lingered in my mind, nor did Johnny offer up the answers that would have given us another chance. My life was set and Johnny knew it. One morning he cornered me. He gave me a kiss and told me that he loved me. I pushed him aside and told him that I was getting married, and I walked out the door. Despite everything, I never doubted his love for me. I just hurt too much to let him back into my life. I had pushed my love for him so far down inside of me I thought it would never survive.

Soon after my marriage, I moved to Louisiana. Johnny stayed around for a year waiting for me to come back. He was convinced that my marriage wouldn't last. After a year of waiting for me this time, he was slipping into a lifestyle that was destroying him. He left the Bay Area and moved up to Washington.

Twenty-two years later, Johnny asked my brother to ask me if I would give him my phone number. At the time, I said no. My marriage was already in deep trouble.

In 2001, my marriage was in its final days. One night I had a very real dream. It was a dream that put me where I am today. I had been asking myself when I had ever really been happy and free from stress. One night I got the answer in a very simple but real dream. I dreamed that I was in a club or a dance hall looking for something and I couldn't find it. I was running out the door crying when I felt arms around me. They were Johnny's arms! I never saw his face or heard his voice. I just knew it was him and I woke up shaking. I tried to push him away again, but he just wouldn't let me be. After this dream, I was haunted by his memory day and night. I had to know where he was and that he was all right. I began to remember so many things but realized that so many memories were lost forever in a cold white fog.

I had no idea where he was. Part of me still suspected Washington. My brother may have mentioned that he lived there. I had no idea how to find out about him, but I knew I needed to try. It took several weeks, but eventually I found out where he was through his brother's wife. I wanted to hear from him, but I wasn't ready for that just yet. I just wanted to know that he was okay; but as soon as he heard that I was looking for him, he asked for my phone number. I didn't get in contact with him until I knew for certain that my marriage was over. Not only was Johnny the love of my life, he was my best friend. I needed my best friend again, so I finally got up the courage to reach out to him.

Johnny never interfered in my life, never asked me to leave my husband and go to him. He often reminded me of what I would be giving up if I left my husband and moved to California. We talked so much, and he supported me. He would constantly remind me of my accomplishments and that because my marriage ended didn't mean that I was a failure.

On my way to my new life in California, I made a side trip to spend some time with Johnny. You can't imagine what it was like to see him again.

There was never one minute of awkwardness between us. It was amazing; it was like we just picked up where we had left off. I was ready for my new life, and was determined to move to California to make a new life for myself. I couldn't stay with him. Maybe someday I could go to him, but not at this time. I needed to keep my relationship with my children. They had to come first. They could never think that I ended my marriage and moved away from them to go to Johnny. That just wasn't true.

It was Father's day, 2002, and I had been in California a little over a month. Johnny called me with some disturbing news. An earlier x-ray and then CT scan had suggested that he might have lung cancer. He ended up in the emergency room because he had trouble breathing. The ER doctor was overworked and very stressed so he gave Johnny some news that he really couldn't be sure of. It was a very cold-hearted way to treat someone, based on an x-ray. He told Johnny that if there was anything he wanted to do, he better do it because he would not be alive in a year. As soon as I heard this news, I dropped everything and made arrangements to go to him.

The third night I was with him, I had to call 911. Later that night, we learned that he had pneumonia, and three days later he was diagnosed with lung cancer. That diagnosis was based on a CT scan that was by then two months old, and a biopsy of one single lymph node in his neck. I was informed of it while he was still in recovery. At the time, I knew very little. The surgeon made the diagnosis before the lab even got the sample. All I was told was that it was stage four non small cell lung cancer. We were never told what kind of non small cell cancer he was supposed to have. I have always suspected that was because the biopsy used for diagnoses was just for show. They seemed to have already made up their minds.

I was with Johnny holding his hand when he was told the news. All he did was squeeze my hand and ask what was next. There was no doubt that he would fight for his life. Later when we were alone, he was very quiet. I asked him what he was thinking, and he told me that he was just trying to figure out what he had done to deserve cancer. I told him that he hadn't done anything bad, that bad things happen to good people.

Johnny was told that he could only have chemotherapy, and no radiation or surgery. When told by the nurse that attitude was ninety percent of the battle, he made up his made that he would win it. He spent four days in the hospital and over two weeks in the rehabilitation unit. I stayed with him night and day. Everyone thought that we were an old married couple. They thought I was putting them on when I told them that not only were we not married, but we had only been together for a few days.

Johnny did very well with the chemotherapy. On the day he had his second treatment, I took him home to an apartment that I had rented for us. We couldn't go to his place because it was eighty miles from his doctor. We suspected that the mobile home he rented played a major role in his illness. It leaked very badly, and you could smell the mold that was growing between the walls.

Our life together was incredible. Neither of us had ever been so happy. All of the hardships in our lives were put aside. We were rewarded with a love that was totally unconditional. I never knew that I could be so happy. Johnny's health improved more everyday. He was having a chemo treatment every week. He never suffered the nausea that you hear so much about. He actually gained thirty pounds. He looked wonderful and everyone who saw him commented on how well he looked. He was so positive that he had everyone convinced that he would beat the cancer. Everyone that is, but the medical staff who was caring for him.

We spent our days just being together. We would go on long rides nearly every afternoon exploring the area where we lived. We drove out to the beach where he had lived and visited with his friends. Once we went to the rain forest and Lake Quinalt. I found wild blackberries and would pick enough each week to make him a cobbler. I loved cooking for him because he had so much appreciation for the food I would fix. He never had anyone take care of him except his mom when he was a small child. Our life together was one of love and mutual respect. It was one of sharing and laughter. We thought that finally we were living the life we had been denied. We just knew we would have years together to make up for the years apart.

One night I was working on some hand sewing and Johnny was sitting next to me watching television. I saw him shake his head so I asked him what was wrong. He replied "Nothing, I was just thinking how perfect this is with you sitting here sewing and the television on. We're a real family. I never knew it could be so good. This is the best that it gets. I have everything I've always wanted."

Johnny loved to snuggle. At night he would be at my back or me at his and wrapping our arms around the other. He would use his feet to draw my legs to him and twine them together with his. We just couldn't get close enough. Sometimes late at night I can close my eyes and still hear him say, "Snuggle my back, honey." He said that we nestled together like a pair of spoons. He just loved to snuggle me so much.

The first series of chemo treatments shrank the cancer fifty percent, possibly more when you consider it was relative to a CT that was two months old. Surely it had grown more before treatment started! On the day he started the second series he ended up in the hospital overnight. He was freezing, with his skin like ice to the touch. Five minutes later he was burning up. I rushed him to the ER. Tests were run but no infection was found. They assumed that he had a reaction to the chemo and decided to drop the Carboplatin. He was still doing very well until one day I asked if he would be given something to replace the Carboplantin. That conversation led to his death.

The hospital just happened to have been overcrowded that day and had put Johnny in a very small room to start his IV. He was claustrophobic. Because of that, he missed the first part of the conversation I had with the nurse. He was busy worrying about being in that small room. When he heard the nurses reply about trying something on the next series of treatments he said that he might not need another series. That is when the nurse made the remark that I know was the beginning of the end. He told Johnny that it didn't matter how good he felt, that he would be on chemotherapy for the rest of his life.

Within twenty-four hours, anxiety became a problem. A week later, when a cold front came through and the wind hit him and took his breath away twice in a short amount of time, he had a panic attack. One attack led to another. His fear of the panic attacks caused anxiety attacks. When we requested medication to help, his doctor refused to give him any, saying he was not having real panic attacks but attacks because he was short of breath. Yet all the tests showed him still improving. The day after the doctor refused the medication, Johnny ended up in the ER with a panic attack so bad that he nearly had a stroke. His release papers stated it was caused by anxiety!

Because he couldn't get anything from his doctor for the anxiety and panic attacks, he started taking the Vicodin that he had been given when first diagnosed, thinking that would help. It didn't take long for him to become addicted. When I would say anything to doctors or nurses I always got the same answer: "What difference does it make? He has lung cancer."

Many times Johnny told me that I was too good to him and that he didn't deserve me or the things I did for him. I told him over and over what a good person he was and that he deserved all I did for him and more. I only hope that I made him realize how true that was.

Two months to the day after the nurse's remark about a lifetime of chemo, Johnny checked himself into the hospital to get help with the anxiety and the addiction to Vicodin. Instead of helping, they increased the amount of the Vicodin he was getting, even though they knew that he didn't have any pain. A respiratory therapist held the nebulizer mask on his face because he kept taking breaks from it. Remember, he was claustrophobic. Finally he went to a nursing home to rest for a week before going home and, I know, to give me a break.

Just a few days before he entered the hospital he had asked me to marry him. He said, "But not now; when I am better. I have a special day all picked out. It is a surprise for you." I know that he was talking about Valentine's Day. He said that was our day because it was a day for lovers and we were true lovers.

While he was in the nursing home I found another treatment center that agreed to help him. We just had to wait until the first of December. When he learned that, his condition turned around again. The only serious problem he had was the Vicodin addiction, but he was confident the new place would help him. Then on Thanksgiving Day, the first day in over two months that he had shown no sign of the anxiety, they decided to give him morphine in a nebulizer. We were told it was for the anxiety. Within two hours he was congested.

The next morning we had planned on him going home. I was concerned about the congestion and had the nurse on duty listen to his chest. She said he had fluids and needed the doctor to see him. Johnny was ready to go home. She delayed for hours calling his doctor. He became more and more agitated and finally I checked him out and was taking him to see the doctor. He started having trouble breathing so I took him to the emergency room. That cost him his life.

They never could find a reason for the congestion but decided that he needed treatment for pneumonia. After several hours, when he was finally calm, they decided to give him a shot of Ativan in his IV. We told them that he had had a bad reaction to it and he refused to take it. The nurse came in a while later and put something in his IV. When we asked what it was she said it was Ativan!

He had a terrible reaction to it. Then a so-called doctor came to his room – not to help him but to harass him because he would not sign a DNR. When Johnny still refused, this guy refused to treat him and made arrangements behind our back to send him to another hospital. Then I was told that I had to leave because they would never get him in the ambulance with me there. I had to find a way to get to where he was going, so to get around Johnny's protests I told him that I was going to the bathroom and left.

The ambulance that was supposed to be on its way didn't get to him for three hours. I found out months later that after I left they gave him morphine again. I knew that after the Ativan he would not have willingly taken anything from them without me there to know what it was. I still can't stand to think about what they must have done to him after I left him there. The next day he remembered nothing except being harassed by that doctor and being given the Ativan. When he got to the other hospital his oxygen was so low they had to work on him. His doctor put a DNR on him without asking and Johnny's son called and made them take it off and treat him.

The next morning he was much better and in a room. His appetite was as good as ever and I knew he was getting better. He just had one problem. His arms would jerk violently when he tried to hold on to anything. Later I learned that was a condition called Myoclonus, caused mostly by drug overdose or a bad reaction to a drug.

That Sunday, December first, a blood gas test was ordered. Johnny's sons and I were told that his blood gases were so bad that they didn't expect him to live through the night. I didn't believe it. He just looked too well and he was still eating and alert. After his sons left they started giving him medication again after saying it would all be stopped unless he asked for it. Later I learned that they had gotten his son on the side and told him that Johnny was dying and the only humane thing to do was give him morphine.

Once they started giving him the morphine and the Vicodin again, the day turned into a nightmare of constant movement. I didn't know at the time that what I was seeing was drug overdose. I just stayed with him and tried to help him. They gave him the last Vicodin that I saw at ten that night. I was stepping outside for a minute while he was on the phone. As I turned to leave he was looking right at me with a sparkle in his eye. I heard him tell his niece that they were saying that he would die in seven days and they were full of shit. Those were the last words I heard him say. When I returned to his room he was sleeping.

After a couple of hours watching him sleep, I decided to try to rest for a while on a sofa down the hall from his room. I had had only four hours sleep in three nights. I told the sitter to call me if there was any change one way or another. I tried but couldn't sleep. I was trying to figure out why he had been acting like he had that day. I was too tired and too worried to sleep so I went back to his room.

He was lying on his left side, a side that he never slept on. His right arm was hanging down the left side of the bed. I remember seeing the orange wrist band with his allergies listed on it, including Ativan. He was just so still that it worried me. I asked the sitter if he was all right and was told that he was fine, just tired from all of the jumping around he had done the night before. When I asked what his vital signs were I was told they hadn't been taken. They didn't want to disturb him. They told me not to disturb him. I listened to them!

I left the room and tried to sleep again but I couldn't get the picture of him out of my mind. I returned to his room. He was in the same position and I was getting more worried. I asked if he was in a coma and was given the same answer as before, "He is just tired, don't disturb him."

Finally they told me that they would wake him at four in the morning and bathe him. I stayed and watched him. He never moved. Finally they came with water and clean clothes. When he was turned over his arms just flopped like a rag doll; still he was bathed and changed. They had put a diaper on him the day before. He was using the urinal but they didn't want to be bothered. They said he wasn't finishing and was wetting the bed. That was a lie. His hand jerked and it spilled. When they took that diaper off, it was dry. I know now that the drugs had shut his kidneys down.

All of the time he was being bathed and his bed was being changed, he was unresponsive. I knew something was wrong but they acted as if it was normal. Then the nurse came in and said that he was barely breathing. That was when she finally took his vital signs. His blood pressure was normal and his heart rate was normal but his oxygen reading was zero. They started running with his bed and when I asked where they were taking him the

145

nurse said to ICU because he was full code and they had to work on him. I knew that he had told them that if he needed it he wanted to be put on a ventilator. I expected to see him on one when they finally let me in to be with him.

When they let me in the room with Johnny, I saw that he was not on a ventilator or awake like I expected him to be. They had bagged him but the nurse was just standing there. She didn't squeeze the bag to force air into his lungs. His oxygen reading was up into the forties but he started gagging on the thing in his mouth so the nurse removed it. Then his oxygen dropped to zero again and I saw his heart start to slow and that is when I knew.

I cried and held his hand and begged him not to leave me. He kicked his legs like he was trying to sit up but his heart got slower and slower as I watched. On December 2, 2002 at 4:55 a.m. I held his hand begging him not to leave me as his life slowly slipped away.

I knew from the first minute it was wrong. Months of research taught me how right I was. Johnny didn't die from lung cancer. He died of the deadly attitude toward lung cancer and drugs that he didn't even need. He was supposed to die to fit their time table and is seems they made sure that he did.

All of those things together and being all alone in a strange place was almost more than I could stand. When unusual things started happening within a day of his death I thought I was doing them and not remembering. It didn't take long for me to realize that I could no longer deny there was more to it than that.

The first night alone in our apartment I was going out of my mind. The pain was so bad and I couldn't get the picture of his fear out of my mind. I was begging for him to help me. I just couldn't stand the thought of his fear. Then while looking for something in his wallet I found a poem that I had written for him before we knew we would be together again. The poem was titled "I'll be there" and told him how at every time and every situation even if we were physically apart that I would be there with him. When I found that poem it was as if

he were using my own words to let me know that he
was there with me and all right.

I'll be there
In the early hours of morning when nature for a new day does
prepare. Close your eyes and think of me and I'll be there

When you walk beside the sea and the wind blows on your face
Think of the one who loves you in a far off distant place

When spring begins in earnest all the world to renew
I'll share in the beauty as I walk beside you

In the long soft days of summer when gentle breezes softly blow
Think of all the love we shared in a time so long ago

May the cool brisk days of autumn with their colors red and gold
Bring thoughts of a love that has never grown old

In the cold brisk days of winter when the sun the clouds do hide
I'll be there to warm you I am always by your side

I pray that when the years have passed and this life grows to an
end. There will be a new life to share our love again

The next morning the poem was gone. I
searched everywhere for it but it was nowhere to be
found. It finally surfaced again nearly a month later,
in a place I had not been since more than a month
before his death.

Arrangements were made for him to be cremated. Because we weren't married yet, I had no say. His sons made the decision and paid for it because Johnny didn't have any insurance. I told them that we had never made any real plans but had spoken about being buried together. But they still chose to have him cremated. His oldest son kept his ashes.

I spoke at his memorial service and I wrote down what I wanted to say so I didn't run the risk of talking too long. Johnny told me that I would be perfect if I just didn't talk so much.

"I met him 44 years ago next month. From the first moment he filled a spot in my heart and touched a spot in my soul that no one else ever could. He taught me how to look at things and people and really see them. He told me that you have to look beyond the surface and see what is deeper to know anyone or anything. That is a lesson I never forgot though we were apart for over 40 years. These past few months he has given me that and so much more. As I stand here today with his family and friends I'm sure you will agree that he had a way about him that you just couldn't forget. Everyone liked him but there were few that he let really know him. I am privileged to say I was not only one of those few but I had the honor to love him and be loved by him. "I know he wasn't perfect but I wouldn't have changed one thing about him. As I told his sons, I think of Johnny as I would a beautiful painting – most have flaws but it is the

flaws that make them unique, priceless, and that is what my Johnny was – priceless. He was a very special man. He was night and day, the calm and the storm. He had a shadow on his heart but a light in his soul. I knew him, and I loved him and every day that we were together, even the bad ones, I found something new to love about him."

By the time I finished I could barely make it back to my seat. I was in so much pain that I nearly collapsed.

There were just so many things to deal with, almost every day. I know my situation was desperate. I was alone and my family didn't know what I was going through. I had no one and all I wanted was to be with Johnny again; to go back and change things so the outcome would be different. My pain was driving me. Nothing else mattered but to prove what had happened to him and then maybe it would be reversed and I could wake up from that nightmare!

There were so many signs and messages that have happened since Johnny passed away. Some of these have been just as dramatic as the following, but there were two that had the biggest impact on me and stand out the most. I wasn't sleeping or eating. Some nights I would sit up until four or five a.m. and then I would be back up by six-thirty or seven. I was living on coffee and nerves, very little else. My situation was getting desperate. My body needed rest and nourishment and I was giving it neither. Then one night something happened to help me sleep. Johnny came to visit me. Like every other night I sat up until the wee hours. I started to doze off and felt hands go around me on my hips and arms. I jumped and looked over my shoulder and Johnny was there. He said, "It's all right, I just want to snuggle you," and I lay down and felt the comfort of his arms around me all night. When I got up the next morning, his robe I slept with was on the far side of the bed nearly falling on the floor instead of at my back where I had put it. There was just enough room between that robe and me for Johnny! Many people would say that because of my stressed condition my mind had just given me a dream to help me. I know that is not true. I have never had a dream before or since that was so vivid. I can still see every detail of it in my mind. Johnny looked exactly as he had the last month of his life; even the black hair showed in his beard, that had appeared so strangely the last day of his life.

After five months of living in that state of limbo I knew that I would have to leave the home we had shared and come back to California. It was a very hard thing for me to do but I was making noise about Johnny's death and finding it impossible to get a job. Before leaving I asked Johnny for one of three signs to let me know that he approved of my leaving and that he would still be with me. I was afraid that if I moved the signs would stop and I would lose him completely. I asked to see or hear a donkey or a rooster or to see a robin. The donkey and rooster had special meaning. The robin I added because I had not seen one since leaving Louisiana. I substituted the rooster for a quail rooster that had made Johnny laugh with its crow.

I ended up finding all of those signs and more once in California. Once I realized that coffee was the one smell I could always associate with him I started smelling it at odd times and in odd places. On the drive from Washington to California my nephew smelled it before I did. We were miles from any settlement. The only explanation was Johnny letting me know he was with me!

I have a pair of praying hands that I wear on a chain around my neck. While Johnny was in the hospital those praying hands became even more important to me. I was living in Southern California for a while. One day after going in and out of several stores I looked down and saw my praying hands were missing. I was desperate to find them but after backtracking the stores I was in and leaving a number in case they were found, I gave up. I never expected to see them again. On the way to my car I started talking to Johnny. I reminded him of how important they were to me and asked him to please help me find them. I was unlocking the door to my car when I just happened to glance down, and there by the side of my car were my praying hands. After that I didn't feel safe wearing them so they stayed on my dresser. When I decided to leave and move up to Northern California I put the praying hands and the chain in the zippered section of my billfold. When I got here the chain was there but not the praying hands. I searched everywhere, even emptying the dust from my vacuum. I opened my suitcase and checked all of the pockets and seams. They were nowhere to be found and I was heartbroken.

Months passed and the second anniversary of Johnny's death was quickly approaching. Thanksgiving Day found me all alone with nowhere to go. I had a weekend job and would have to leave early the next morning. That date was the anniversary of a very painful day, Johnny's last hospital stay. Like that day had been, it was cold, foggy and a light rain was falling. I was very depressed. I decided to pack for my job early in the day just to have something to do. I took my suitcase out of the closet and lay it on my bed. When I opened it I couldn't believe my eyes. There in the middle of the suitcase laying face up were my praying hands! I had searched that suitcase more than once. I had even used it after my move. Those praying hands had not been there. Even had they somehow been stuck in a seam and I missed them when that suitcase had been set on end, they would have fallen to the other end. There is no EARTHLY way they got into that suitcase. I felt Johnny at that moment and knew that he was giving me something special to get me through a very rough time.

I lost the praying hands once again after that and found them again just as mysteriously. It has been nearly four years since that terrible day that I lost my Johnny. My life has changed and I have grown in many ways. The signs don't come as often as they did but I still get them when I really need them.

Today I was driving a client out in the country. We were going up to see the salmon at the fish hatchery. The autumn leaves are in full color just as they were four years ago today when Johnny and I went on a beautiful drive out in the country. I was enjoying my day but in the back of my mind and deep in my heart was the old pain. The memories and anniversaries are always a reminder. For some reason we went further on a different road just sightseeing. I decided to turn around in a driveway by a pasture, and when I looked up there was a donkey! Later on my walk I flushed a whole covey of quail.

I never believed people could communicate with us after they died. I lost my mom and dad and three brothers but never experienced anything like that until I lost my Johnny. The bond between us is just too strong to break. It is strong enough that it survived over forty years of separation and it survives the death of his body. Some day we will be together again. I have no doubts about that. When that day comes we really will have come full circle.

In Loving Memory of

Johnny Fields

March 15, 1933 – December 2, 2002

By: Lilian Duplantis

Lorraine

I remember I was at work when my grandmother called me. I'm not sure of the exact month but I remember what she said and what she sounded like as if it was yesterday. "Oh Lisa? It's Grandma; the doctor found a spot on my lung!" I stood there and felt sick knowing Grandma was a longtime smoker. As I asked her what the doctor was going to do and if he was doing a biopsy she began to cry. I felt helpless and told her it would be all right, we would help her. I was married at the time and called my husband crying. Although there has for some time been tension between my family and my husband, he understood and was sympathetic, swearing to me Grandma was going to be all right. I wish he were right!

Her biopsy came back saying it was lung cancer, and it was recommended she do chemo and radiation treatments. The whole family seemed to come together to help my grandma. I had two small children and one on the way and was unable to get to her house as much as

I wanted to, but I called her every day. She told me of her pain and the difficulty breathing; by now she decided she wanted to stop smoking. Nice time to decide, once she was diagnosed with lung cancer!

My sister, stepmother, father, aunt, uncle and her friend Harold all took turns taking her to her appointments taking care of her needs including her pain meds. As she became weaker, it was harder to understand what she was saying. She became incredibly ill from the chemo which was supposed to make her better. I would like to know when the scientists can finally come up with something that actually helps and does not make it worse! Why do you have to get worse before getting better?

I saw this woman who used to ask me upon every visit if she had lost weight, as she was now so frail. Grandma, like everyone, had shrunk with age. She was once 5' 8" tall and weighed maybe 105 to 120, and now at the age of 76 she was about 5' and weighed 125 to 130.

We saw her whittle away to almost nothing, maybe 90 pounds.

She tried to live as normal a life as she could. She went to dinners with Harold, still had my dad and uncle over every morning and their coffee ready just in time for them to arrive, a daily tradition spanning thirty years. She even made it to Christmas at my uncle Don's, showing up looking great with the minor exception of no hair and little energy. My daughter who was shy from birth and now almost two years old was warming up to her and she smiled. My grandma lived for these kids!

She brought this head turban to show off her style, laughing as she put it on her head; she took it off, though, saying she preferred not to wear it, and so she rarely did. By this time her hair had begun to grow back in. It was a bit on the fuzzy side so she laughed about it and said she thought it was coming in curly and blonde. She saw it how she wanted; it was still very short with no curl and was coming in silver. But I loved it!

Almost a year has passed now and I got another phone call at work; it was Grandma. She was so happy and excited! She said, "Oh Lisa? The doctor said the cancer is gone! He said there is no sign of it!" I felt so relieved and asked what now, and asked how many more treatments. She said her doctor who was way past retirement and in his early 90's said she doesn't need any more chemo or radiation. I asked her to get another opinion but she trusted him.

A month or so later she called me and said the cancer was back. Not only had it grown, rapidly engulfing her one lung, but it had also spread to her other lung! I talked to the doctor I worked with and got his recommendation for a new oncologist. I set up an appointment for her and my sister took her in for her consult and was informed the cancer was back and very aggressive, now moreso then before. We were all so shocked, after the other doctor had said she was in remission! More treatments, MRIs, x-rays, medication, radiation and the horrible chemo. She was on so many pain meds and got more and more weak and delirious.

One of the medications made her so "silly" as she called it, that as she tried to get up to go to the bathroom she lost her balance and fell, hitting her head on the night stand next to the bed and cutting her head open. She had to be taken to the emergency room by ambulance to get stitches. It was unclear how many pills she had taken; the blood tests showed an overdose so we thought that maybe she forgot she had already taken her meds. We will never know. Witnessing this was something I don't ever want to witness again in my life; I pray none of my loved ones ever have to go through it.

Seeing her go through this ordeal made me believe more in the angels and spirits than I ever have in my life. On one of my visits to Grandma's, she asked me to go talk to the people peeking at her from behind her tree. I told her I didn't see anyone there, but she insisted, so I went outside to check and no one was there. She said there were two people there, and they would wave and smile at her. She just wanted to talk to them and invite them in for coffee. I told her not to be letting anyone in; she was always so friendly to others. I believe those were spirits trying to help her with what was coming and to help guide her into the afterlife. I find comfort in that.

By now her smoking had started back up. She said it was too late to quit now and laughed that very familiar laugh, now a bit rough and weak. She told me she had to live through this because she had to see her grandbabies grow up. She said she couldn't give up! She was slowly getting worse, not better, however, and I think she knew she was dying. She began talking about her mother and how much she missed her and wanted to see her again, and how much she wanted to see my grandfather.

Easter was approaching and she wanted everyone to come over. She said she couldn't get out, so we should come to see her. By now my baby was born and we named her Sarah. My grandma was thrilled since her mother's name was Jennifer Sarah. I had no idea! The name just fit her when I saw her. There were about twenty people there at a minimum and she was so happy about that. My sister Susan helped Grandma get ready. She brought Grandma outside in her wheelchair wearing a pink and purple jumpsuit with an afghan across her lap, and to top it all off she was wearing slippers that were crocheted for her with fuzzy pompoms on them, and a yellow bow on her head. She laughed that weak rough laugh and had the biggest smile on her face! It was the most wonderful sight and the happiest moment we had with her in a long time. She sat as the kids all searched for their eggs, then got too tired to sit outside any longer, so she went in to rest. The party went on per her request until dusk.

I went back down to Grandma's a few days later with my family. My brother and his wife were there and my sister as well, who by now had quit her job to take care of Grandma. She lived forty-five minutes away but every day, twice a day and sometimes even more, she drove to Omaha to care for our dying grandmother. My sister became a saint during this time, carrying the load of her care.

My Grandma began to cry this night; she said how much she missed her mom and my Grandpa who had been gone for twenty-three years. I told her I would like a picture of her holding my baby; she smiled and gladly moved her arms as much as she could. I laid Sarah across her arms and took the last picture I would ever take of her.

Once Nick and my brother-in-law returned from getting food, she kept looking at Nick and saying "Joe, that was sure nice of you to bring Lisa and the kids down." Joe was my stepdad, and my husband Nick looked at me and I shook my head slightly; he knew I meant "don't correct her" and politely said, "That's my pleasure Lorraine, anything for you." My sister was making liver and onions for Grandma. None of us liked it but it was always one of her favorite foods. We were eating steaks when Grandma said, "How do you like that liver, Lisa?" I just looked at her and said it was the best I have ever eaten, and told her Susan really knows how to cook liver! She smiled and took one more bite and fell asleep.

A few days later Susan took her to the doctor for her latest chest x-ray. The doctor sent her to drain her lungs again but there was nothing to drain. Her lungs by now had been almost fully engulfed by the cancer, leaving no hope. She had to be admitted and placed on an oxygen mask, and we were told she would never have the chance to take that mask off again.

I went up to the hospital to see her that evening with my mother. She looked so tired and just fed up with what she was dealing with. My mom and I helped her into the chair that was given to her to go to the bathroom. That was the first time I saw exactly how thin she was. She was very light and had no muscle mass leaving her with no strength. Once she was done and we helped get her back into bed, Mom cried and commented that she had known my grandma longer then she had known her own mother. Mom said she loved my grandma like she was her mom and said she couldn't let her go; she wasn't ready either.

The next day I received a call in my office from my dad. I felt like throwing up when he told me to get up to see Grandma because it didn't look like she was going to make it another day. The nurse said she had the familiar "breath of death," as it was put to me. I broke down crying and was walked up to her room by a friend of mine. When I arrived at her room I was told she was in a coma and didn't feel any more pain. Do the doctors and nurses really know that she isn't hurting anymore? Why do they tell you this if they don't know?

I spent an hour and a half by her side talking to her and telling her I loved her. Watching her chest rise with such a struggle and drop so hard, it was evident she was fighting to stay alive! As I said before, she was such a fighter and wasn't willing to go yet. I told her that it was okay to go home to her mom and Grandpa, and that we would be okay. I said I would never forget her and would always love her to the day I see her in Heaven.

I prayed to my Grandpa to come get her so she isn't alone when she leaves, and I asked that her mom meet her when she gets to Heaven. I told her friend Harold that I was going to my office to shut off my computer and sign out, and then I went back to her and kissed her, telling her again that I loved her and that it was okay to let go. Then I left to go to my office.

I walked into my office and to my desk and the phone rang. It was my sister-in-law Brianna. She said, "Lisa, she's gone." I said, "What!" and told her, I just left her, she can't be gone, and that I was on my way up to her.

She can't be gone yet, I thought; I wasn't there with her! Apparently my sister and brother were just walking into the room when she drew her last breath. As I walked up to her room and walked in, she was lying there so peacefully for the first time in a year. She was so cold and silent. All I could do was cry and hold her hand. Her funeral was three days later, the same date my sister had been married. That was the most difficult day. I think we all were in such shock. Let's just say the beer went fast at the reception!

A week later I was still crying occasionally, especially since I just got my pictures back from Easter. My husband was working and my kids were asleep when I decided to look at the pictures. I got to the one of Grandma with her pink pompoms on her feet and laughed, saying, "I miss you Grandma" – then suddenly there was an overwhelming smell of cigarette smoke! This was odd since I don't smoke and my husband wasn't home. The smell was so strong in my room where my two little girls were; I couldn't get past it. I said "Grandma? Is that you?" Then the smell faded. This occurred off and on for about three weeks, and only when I was upset. My husband had said he thought he saw her in the bathroom mirror, and I dismissed it thinking he was nuts. I now believe him.

The oddest thing I have experienced since her death seven years ago happened about the time of my divorce. The overwhelming smell of cigarette smoke again flooded my apartment. I was so depressed at this time, asking for Grandma to help me get through this as she had always done in the past. This smell didn't go away for a few minutes. My two oldest were at school and my youngest was taking a nap on the couch, so I thought it a perfect opportunity to pack. As I packed up some dishes, I heard, "Oh Lisa?" in that old familiar voice. I stood there and cried. I have never shared that with anyone until now. There *is* life after death.

I have now been divorced for four years and have dealt with it very well. My latest challenge is upon me with the child support now stopped. I thought of Grandma and all that she has endured. Once again the smell of cigarette smoke lingered in the air. This time my daughters asked me who was smoking in the house. I replied that nobody is smoking in here and said I think my grandma is saying hi. My girls just smiled and said hi to their great-grandmother who fought so hard to see them grow.

I think my grandma is trying to tell us she is here for us, and although she can't be here in body she will be here in spirit. I find it comforting to know she is out there, beautiful, and is no longer in pain. I miss you, Grandma, and will always love you!

In Loving Memory of

Lorraine M. Chamberlain-Lakin

September 3, 1922 – April 8, 1999

By: Lisa Neff

Play it again Daddy

When I was eleven, I thought everything would always be okay, until my father was shot and killed for a wallet that only held enough for him to get a pack of cigarettes.

Things were very hard after that. My mom slept most of the day away because she worked nights at a local Walgreens. When you walked into my house, you couldn't tell that my father ever had lived there anymore. My mother had either sold or thrown away most of his things. She told me that seeing his things around the house would make her cry. I said I didn't mind, but only if she kept the medium-sized piano that my grandfather had made for my dad when he was seven. My mother said all right, but we had to keep it in the basement. I was so very happy because my father would always sit me on his lap before bed, and he would play "Mary Had a Little Lamb." I had even named it "Daddy's piano."

One night my mother went to work at around 10 o'clock at night. It was Friday, so I stayed up until midnight, and then I went to bed. I was just about to fall asleep when I heard music playing softly. Thinking it was just my imagination, I tried to go back to sleep, but the music would not go away. I was so scared at that moment that I grabbed my pillow and blanket, ran into my mother's room, and fell asleep. I woke up the next morning and ate breakfast. I thought it was odd that she didn't ask me why I slept in her bed, but I thought nothing of it really.

The music would not go away. Every Friday when my mom went to work, I would hear the music and end up sleeping in my mom's bedroom. One Friday after my mom had left for work, I decided that when the music began to play I would find out where it was coming from. I sat in my bed until around twelve-thirty, and then I heard the music. I got up from my bed and began to look everywhere. I remembered Daddy's piano downstairs in the basement. I crept downstairs, feeling very afraid. I stopped when I reached the bottom stairs. There, sitting at the piano was a light.

I was so afraid until I realized the song; it was "Mary Had a Little Lamb." At that moment, all my fear was washed away, and only the best feelings were the ones I felt. I remember saying "Daddy? Is that you?" When I asked that question, I had a strong feeling as if everything was going to be okay. Then the music stopped and the light disappeared. I then walked upstairs and into my room and I fell asleep. I have never told my mother what happened because I was sure that she would not have believed me. Do you know what? Life did get better. My mom got a much better job, and she met and married a really nice guy. I will always remember that time in the basement, and I will always remember my dad and how he made me feel so happy. I love you, Dad.

Written by: Marie .M, Indiana, USA

Submitted by: Castle of Spirits

www.castleofspirits.com

Tony

Ever since I was a little girl, I had always wanted a Pug dog. I have always loved dogs, and there hasn't been a moment in my life when I've not owned at least one dog.

One day, when I was twelve years old, I was at a neighbor's house only two doors down from my house when my mom called to say she was coming home from running some errands. "I have a friend of mine with me I'd like you to meet," she said. "His name is Tony." I thought it a bit odd at the time, but when she finally got home she came over to our neighbor's house with a little off-white ball of fur in her arms. A tiny head with big eyes and a scrunched-up nose poked out, sniffing the air. This was the friend, a Pug puppy named Tony. Right then and there I fell in love with that tiny, round little puppy! Oh, was he cute.

Turns out, he was born the day after my twelfth birthday, so we always included Tony in my parties. He soon became my best friend, watching TV with me before bed and sitting outside with me as I swam in the pool. One day, I had gotten out of the pool and was heading for the door inside when I heard a splash! Tony had rounded a corner too fast and had fallen in the deep end of the pool. We rarely let him swim unless someone was right there with him, mainly due to his pushed-in nose. Without a second thought I dropped my towel and plunged into the pool, pulling Tony out in time. I don't think he ever forgot that.

Our house had a potted patch of yellow flowers outside, next to our door into the kitchen from the backyard; they looked a lot like pretty yellow daisies. Every once in a while I would go out and find the nicest one, come back inside with the yellow flower, and say, "I have a flower for Tony!" and stick it in his kennel with him. Tony would sniff it a bit, and then try to eat it. "No, no, no," I'd laugh. "You don't eat the flower, Tony!"

One night in June of this year I stayed up late, watching TV as six-year-old Tony sat next to me. Finally, at one in the morning, I decided it was time for bed, since I was to go to the movies with a friend the next morning. I told Tony to get in his kennel for the night, and he did; I crouched down next to the door to give his ear a scratch when something told me to call him out again, so I did. I played with him for a few minutes, giving him a big hug and a kiss. He was so happy and playful. When he got back in his kennel I closed him up and said, "You're my good boy, Tony. I love you." With that, I went to bed. The next morning my mother called up to me at about eight-thirty. I could detect a slight worry and panic in her voice despite the fact she was keeping her cool as best she could. "Ginny," she called, "I think Tony's sick!"

"Well, okay," I thought. "Maybe he's just sick to his stomach. Nothing medicine can't cure, right?" Unfortunately no. When I went into the kitchen, where Tony and our Chocolate Lab slept at night, the smell just about knocked me out. Tony wasn't in his kennel; he had gotten sick all over the kitchen floor. Maneuvering across the kitchen, I rounded the corner and into the utility room to find Tony lying on the floor, panting and foaming at the mouth. He was in a waking coma. Mom and I wrapped him in towels; my mom had called the vet, with whom we were friends. She owns a bunch of pugs as well. She told us to bring Tony in immediately, and said that she would be waiting for us.

So the two of us leapt into the car: Mom drove, and I held Tony in my lap, talking to him. I started thinking that this might be his last ride in the car. He always loved rides in the car. We dropped Tony off at the veterinarian's, and rode home in silence. My friend's dad picked me up a short while later, and I told my friend what was happening.

We still went to the movies, and after the second one was over I checked my phone messages. Mom had called, and she told me that Tony had died at the vet's office. There was no chance for him. We were thinking he had gotten into something poisonous. I couldn't help but sit down and bawl my eyes out, right there in the middle of a crowded mall.

The pain never went away after that. We sent him to College Station, where Texas A & M University is located, to have an autopsy done on him to help determine cause of death. My mom and

I had to drive out to pick up his body in a cooler inside a cardboard box. Right after he died the vet had taken his paw and made a paw print in clay for us, and also taken a clipping of his fur from behind his little ear. We had Tony cremated, and his remains now lie in a little wooden box on my windowsill along with the fur clipping. The paw print and Tony's collar are also with it.

About a week after he died, it was still so hard for us to even think about him without crying. Then something very odd happened. One morning I woke up and forgot that Tony had died. I was thinking about needing to feed him, and then I remembered that he was gone. I pulled myself out of bed anyway, trying not to cry. When I looked down as I got out of my bed, someone had dropped a yellow daisy right by my bed. I checked my door and it was locked from the inside. My younger brother had spent the night at a friend's house, and my mom's room was downstairs and on the other side of the house.

There was no way that daisy could have gotten there, but it brought me great comfort.

By Virginia, eighteen years old

Submitted by: Castle of Spirits

www.castleofspirits.com

Tiffany

I was walking through the courtyard to church on Sunday morning, when I noticed quite a few people looking sad, and some even crying. One of the girls from high school youth group, where I volunteered as a counselor, ran over to me and asked if I had heard what happened. I said no, because I had only just arrived. She said that Tiffany was hit by a truck the day before and was in critical condition at Children's Hospital. At first I didn't make the connection as to who she was. I knew she must be a kid, because some young girls were huddled nearby and crying.

I talked with the girl for a while, and then proceeded into the church to sit in my usual pew. As I waited for church to start, I lost myself in thought. I had a vision, for lack of a better word. I saw an African American girl and she was holding something like a blanket or a stuffed animal close to her. She was walking toward three people, all in white robes. Two were elderly men, one with very silver, wavy hair parted on the side. The other I didn't see very well, but I knew he was an elderly man. The third person was a short black woman, with her hair pulled tight into a bun on the crown of her head. I know this seems cliché, but that is what I was seeing. The man with wavy hair and the black woman were smiling and beckoning the girl toward them. She seemed very happy to see the woman, and was smiling as she walked toward her.

At that moment I knew who Tiffany was. She was only 12 years old, too young to be in the high school youth group, but she had helped out in my son's Bible class. I thought it was so odd that I had had this vision, because though her older brother was in youth group, her parents were only acquaintances of mine, and I didn't know her very well at all.

This vision was very clear, as if it was happening right in front of me. Then I felt as if I couldn't breathe. I felt as if a strong fan had started in front of my face, causing me to almost gasp for breath. I'm not sure I am explaining it well, but I felt as if I was just gasping. My husband Bill turned to me and asked if I was okay. His voice kind of woke me up, making me look around and try to focus on where I was. It was the oddest feeling I had ever experienced.

While the pastor was making his opening announcements, he was passed a note. He began telling the congregation that Tiffany had just passed away. Her parents and two brothers were with her at the hospital and he had just received the news. I was in shock. I knew what had just happened. I had witnessed, if you will, Tiffany's passing.

But why me? Why was I chosen to see this? I had always been open to this sort of thing, but it had never happened to me. I had heard stories about things like this happening to other people, but never me. There are always the occasional wacky people who claim to see things, or maybe make something supernatural out of a coincidence, or try to piece little things together to make situations into something more than they are. But this was different. It happened, plain as day, and then it was over. Just like that. Or so I thought.

The next few days were so strange. I kept having memories of the vision in my head. I couldn't get rid of them. They were so strong. It wasn't more of the actual vision, just memories of it. There was such a tugging for me to tell Tiffany's mother Debbie about the vision. Of course I thought she would think I was nuts, so I kept it to myself. I didn't tell anyone at all for about three months.

For those months the tugging and nagging in my head were almost unbearable. "Tell Debbie, tell her. She needs to know." It sounds so very odd, but that is what the voice kept saying . . . every day, and often. I was in college earning my degree at the time and was finding it hard to study. I wasn't obsessed – quite the opposite. I was trying to ignore it, thinking if I did, it would stop, but it never did. I would wake up in the night to the nagging, "Tell her, tell her."

I don't have any family history of telepathic gifts, or of schizophrenia for that matter, but this was driving me nuts! I was unable to concentrate on my studies and was losing sleep.

But what was I to do, go and tell Debbie, a woman I barely knew that I had a vision about her daughter that had just been killed in a horrible accident? She was going through enough without some nut telling her she had a vision of her daughter. She didn't know me very well, either, so I was sure she would want to have me committed, or maybe she would just think I was playing a cruel joke. But then again, I couldn't sleep and couldn't concentrate, so I decided I needed to say something.

The next Sunday at church, I called Debbie into a stairwell. I told her that I was so sorry about Tiffany, and that I realized that there were no words anyone can say to make the death of a child even slightly better. I knew this and didn't want to even try.

Then I told her what I guess anyone with this kind of news would. "Please don't think I am crazy, I am not. I have been trying to understand this myself, but there is only one explanation. I had a vision, a real vision." I tried to explain to her what had happened that morning while I was a church sitting in the pew, when she was at the hospital bedside of her daughter right before she passed away. The words just came pouring out, every detail. How Tiffany had been carrying something, like a stuffed animal or blanket close to her, the older black woman with her hair pulled tight in a bun, the old man with the wavy hair, and the other old man that I couldn't really see. All in white robes and smiling. How they were beckoning Tiffany toward them and she was happy to see the woman.

Right when I said that, Debbie started crying, and I mean really crying hard. She reached over and hugged me so tight and cried for a long, long time. Finally she pulled back and thanked me profusely. She said that she had had no signs at all, and was waiting for something to tell her that her daughter was okay. She believed that the older black woman I described was Tiffany's grandmother who had died only a few months prior. She and Tiffany were very close, and Tiffany was devastated when she died.

Debbie knew her daughter was in good hands and she felt some relief. She didn't know who the older man with wavy hair was, and I had no description for the other man, but she seemed so content and happy that her daughter was with her beloved grandmother.

To be honest, Debbie wasn't the only one feeling relieved. When we finally left the stairwell, I had the best feeling ever. I had such a huge weight lifted from me. I felt like I could fly . . . no more tension, no more stress, only pure euphoria. After that day, Debbie and I became closer friends.

I found out later that though they had planned on burying Tiffany, they ended up cremating her and placing her ashes next to the ashes of her grandmother. I don't know if it had anything to do with my conversation with Debbie, but it seemed to bring closure to the family at such a devastating time in their lives.

A book I read recently talked about guardian angels, and said that everyone had three. I guess Tiffany's angels were caring for her at the most needed time. I never actually believed in guardian angels before, but after what I experienced that day at church sitting in that pew, I certainly do now.

By: Eva Urick

Sita

I had another similar experience a couple of years later. I worked for a commercial printer as the Art Director, and one of the Customer Service Reps was a wonderful girl named Sita. I found her fascinating and extremely intelligent. We became fast friends and I immediately felt very close to her. She and her husband, Dan, were high school sweethearts and soul mates. They were very young when they got married, and though most marriages fitting this scenario usually don't work, theirs was the strongest I had ever seen. They had a lovely young daughter and were pregnant with their second child – a boy this time.

It was fun to see someone so happy and glowing with the anticipation of a baby. She endured a lot of teasing because of her big belly, whining because of her back, all of it. We were not a delicate bunch, and before long she knew for sure her butt was big, she was busting out of her shirts and we were all jealous, and we all stepped aside with exaggeration when she walked by us down the hall. She was so cute in every way. She was petite with big brown eyes, beautiful thick hair, and a smile that could light up any room. She always had a little skip to her step and was always willing to help out in any way she could.

But one day when she was in her eighth month, she came to work looking very pale. I asked how she was feeling, and she said fine; but I could tell she wasn't, and just didn't want to worry anyone. I asked when her next doctor appointment was, and she said later that day. I was very worried, and had a really awful feeling. She had rings around her eyes and was so pale she looked almost blue. I asked if the baby was keeping her up at night by kicking her. She said no; he had been pretty quite lately. Then I really started worrying. I told her to call the doctor and see if he could take her earlier. She said her appointment was at 11 a.m. and she was leaving in an hour anyway, so would just wait a bit.

We got a call at about 11:30 from Dan. He had met her at the doctor and they had just heard the news that their baby boy had died. They were going to induce labor the next day. Needless to say, Sita and Dan were shattered. They would have been the best parents, and that baby boy would have had the most loving and fun parents any one could ask for. We were so sorry for them both, but also for us. We were looking so forward to having a baby who no doubt would be visiting the office often.

The cards and flowers came pouring in, but it would never take the place of Sita's baby boy. I called her every couple of days while she was out of work and she sounded so depressed. She felt that it was her fault that the baby died. I suppose this is normal under the circumstances. Tests revealed no explanation, but she still felt so guilty. She was miserable and nothing but time would make things better.

A few nights later, I had another vision. I wasn't scared this time, I just let it take hold of me. I saw Sita sitting in a chair in a hospital with her hair tied back in a ponytail. She was holding a baby boy and she was so happy. I was standing behind her and could see only the side of her face, and she was smiling and cooing at the baby. There was no sign of the baby being a boy, but I just knew it was. But it wasn't the same baby that had just passed. It was a different one.

Then I heard a voice that said that the baby she was holding was one that was waiting for her – a healthy baby boy. The baby that she lost was not her fault, it was just not his time. But there was a healthy baby boy waiting for her, and I needed to tell her this.

I came out of the vision without interruption – just came out of it. I wasn't scared and I wasn't going to wait this time and inflict the torment on myself and more importantly, Sita and Dan.

I went to work the next day and asked Sita to join me for lunch. I was working at the different office that day and asked her to meet me at a restaurant we both knew. She agreed. Once we got there and sat down, I started right in. First, I briefly told her about the first vision I had had with Tiffany. Then I told her that I had also had a vision about her and the baby. I explained the whole vision to her and told her that the baby she lost was not her fault at all, that it just wasn't his time. There was nothing she did or could have done to prevent this, it was just not his time. She started crying, but also was relieved to hear this. She had been waiting for some sign from anyone to explain the situation.

I then told her that there was a healthy baby boy waiting for her. She was going to have a healthy baby boy. She told me the doctor told her to wait a while before she should start trying again. I told her I didn't know when the time was ready for her physically, I only knew that there was a baby boy waiting for her. She seemed so happy and relieved, but again, she was not the only one – I was thrilled that I didn't wait to tell her. I could not have endured the nagging and tugging I went through with the previous vision, and I certainly didn't want my friend to suffer any more than needed.

About 18 months later Sita had a beautiful, healthy baby boy. At this point I was no longer working at the same company, but Sita and I emailed and talked often. We kept in very close touch, as we had shared such an intimate moment. She sent pictures of the kids and I could tell they all were so very happy. What a gorgeous family.

About two years later I received a phone call from our mutual friend and co-worker, Jesse. He said to sit down, and that he had horrible news and wanted to call me himself. Sita and Dan were in New York for Dan's father's funeral. They were on the way to the funeral and were in a car accident and both were killed. These young, beautiful people – killed just like that. I was in shock. I couldn't breathe. My friend with whom I had shared a unique bond was gone. The next few days were very sad and depressing,

Then I had the best feeling – I felt and smelled Sita breeze through me. I breathed in deep and it was the unmistakable smell of her, right through me. I had the feeling that I should contact her stepmother and tell her that she and Dan were okay. It was so weird. It wasn't a vision, just a feeling, and such a strong smell and presence of Sita. I didn't know her stepmother, or anyone in her family for that matter. I had only met Dan and the kids.

So I decided I would talk to her at the funeral. I went, but for some reason I sensed that she wasn't there. So I found Sita's sister, whom I had also never met, but she looked so much like Sita, they could have been twins. I asked her if her stepmother was there, and she said no. I gave her a piece of paper with my phone number on it and told her it was really important that she give this to her stepmother. She said ok, but was so distraught, I didn't think she would remember.

Two days later I got a phone call from Lorri, Sita's stepmother. Sita's sister never gave her my number, but Sita had told her about me and she also had the feeling she should talk to me. So she looked in Sita's cell phone for my number. I told her about the feeling that I had had and the smell and the presence of Sita. I told her that Sita and Dan were okay. She talked to me for a long time on the phone about how she had been with them right before they died. They were walking through the woods by Dan's family's home in New York, talking about Dan's mother now having to live without his father. Sita and Dan both agreed that they would never want to live without each other. I guess that is now set in stone.

When Sita lost her baby, she wrote this beautiful poem, and asked me to do something with it so she could frame it. After fluffing it up with a nice background, I kept it on file. I think she would love to share it with anyone who has gone through the same or similar situation.

The sun shines strong upon my face
On those days when it seems lonely in this place.

I feel it's you looking down on me,
Your best friend is the great and almighty

It gives me strength in times of need,
Allowing love and energy
For those who remain here with me.
I will never forget your beautiful face,
That of my son, I will never replace.

There is a piece of my heart,
That will wait an eternity to be with you.
— Sita Koletar

I am not telepathic, I can't read the future and I can't control these visions or feelings, but I have always had an open mind. For me these visions just happen. I think they happen to many people. Some people choose to accept them with an open mind and others choose to shut them out.

In Loving Memory of

Sita Koletar

September 28, 1977 – July 31, 2003

By: Eva Urick

Dennis

In 1977, Dennis and I were introduced through a mutual friend. We realized right away that we were soul mates. We were married four months after meeting, and one year later, our son was born. I had two very young children from a previous marriage that Dennis took right under his wing, becoming the father that they had never had. He was such a wonderful father and our life was good.

Dennis was a master plumber and his pride was the company he started and ran for twelve years. Life was going so great. The boys were getting older and life was slowing down a bit. Our oldest son graduated from law school and began practicing law. Our youngest was in college and our middle son was doing well at his job. He was so involved in life. Everyone that met Dennis automatically loved him, and he had so many friends. He loved cars, astronomy, ham radio . . . just to mention a few. He loved everything associated with the space program and rarely missed a launch.

Dennis never complained or even indicated that he felt bad. There were no symptoms of what was to soon change our lives completely. After catching a bug, Dennis went to our family doctor for antibiotics. The doctor ordered a routine chest x-ray. I will never forget the day I learned the results. I was at work when I received the call from Dennis. I was standing by a wall-mounted phone and as I heard the words, I slowly slid to the floor with only the wall supporting me. Dennis was diagnosed with small cell lung cancer. At the time of diagnosis the cancer was present in both lungs, the liver and the spine. Dennis was only 49 years old. How could this be happening?

For ten months, very aggressive treatment was administered. Dennis and his oncologist, Dr. Omar Kayalah, from M. D. Anderson in Orlando, formed a very special bond. I don't think Dennis would have made it as long as he did if it hadn't been for the support and care of Dr. Kayalah.

Dennis passed away in a hospital bed in the bedroom we shared. He passed away in the very early hours of Sunday morning, December 15, 2002. I was with him, holding his hand, when he peacefully passed. My best friend was the first person to arrive at my house and she made all of the necessary calls for me. I remained in the room with Dennis, not able to leave his side.

My friend and daughter-in-law had stepped outside for a few minutes and then the excitement began. Suddenly, everyone was calling for me to come outside. I replied that I didn't want to leave Dennis. The hospice nurse then came into the room and told me that I would forever regret not going outside if I didn't come. When I got outside, many of my neighbors were lining my street to see this amazing thing happening. Just over the roof above where Dennis was lying in our room, there were thousands of little birds that were just hovering right over the house. These birds seemed to have come from nowhere. Someone identified them as "swifts." I have never seen so many birds in one place at one time. These little birds remained, hovering over the exact area where Dennis was, until the transport van came to take his body away. Then, the birds left, following that van all the way to the mortuary. I believe this was Dennis' way of letting me know he was "as free as a bird" and had joined their ranks. Dennis left this earth, escorted by a flock of thousands of tiny birds.

In Loving Memory of
Dennis King

May 10, 1952 - December 15, 2002

By: Ann King

Elizabeth

This is a mother's story. It is a story of love, life, loss and new life. But the greatest of these is love. This is my story.

It all began on September 12, 1983 . . . the day my world forever changed and I learned what love was all about. It was the day that Elizabeth Jean came into my life; the day my oldest daughter was born.

The two most painful days of my life have revolved around my Elizabeth, or Liz, as she prefers to be called. September 12, 1983 was the most physically painful day of my life. After 24 hours of excruciating labor, and finally a c-section, my beautiful daughter came into the world.

She was the cutest, most adorable baby I had ever seen. She had a massive head of wild black hair and the biggest blue eyes ever. She was less than an hour old when my parents came to see their first grandchild. I will always remember my dad telling me, with tears streaming down his face, how he looked into the nursery, and she lifted up her head and looked right at him, as if to say, "Here I am, Grandpa." Oh yes, she was special, our little Elizabeth.

She made our life "interesting" for the next twenty years. She was so full of life. You never knew what she would do or say. I was in awe of her. She was everything I always wanted to be, but never was. Until she reached the age of 17 . . . and suddenly it seemed that our beloved daughter became someone I didn't know or understand. People talk about "hell on earth" and I so know what they mean. Hell for me was having a daughter that I loved more than anything, but who fell into the traps of smoking, drinking and always living on the edge. She had absolutely no intention of listening to anyone, especially to either of her parents. All we could do was stand by and watch it all unfold. If our love could have saved her, she would still be here.

The most emotionally painful day of my life was September 20, 2003 – the day my beautiful daughter left the physical world and entered into spirit. But as painful as that was, the minute I knew it had happened, I knew she was okay and that she was being taken care of, as was I, by a God whose love knows no bounds. He accepted my daughter with love, and showered a love and peace on me that I will never fully comprehend or be able to explain. But, it is there and it is as real as the sun that shines and the rain that falls. For love never dies, it is eternal.

It was June 7, 2001. My heart raced excitedly as our car exited the airport, and I breathed a huge sigh of relief. We had just dropped off our 17-year-old daughter, Liz, and two of her friends. They were headed out on a much-anticipated trip to France and Spain, coordinated by one of the foreign language teachers at their high school.

I was decidedly giddy as I thought of a three-week hiatus from my very headstrong, determined oldest daughter. I loved her more than anything, but she had tried our patience as parents so many times. We were almost always beside ourselves with worry and fear, wondering, why does she do the things she does? She was insistent on always living on the edge, constantly testing us, and nearly always defying our authority.

Deep down, I was very worried, but I didn't know how to make her change, or see that her behavior was so self-destructive. Naively I thought, any day now, she'll see the error of her ways and change. She'll run to me and exclaim, "Oh Mom, how could I have been so crazy; you were so right." But every night seemed to bring the same thing; out with her friends till all hours, smoking, drinking, and God only knows what else.

Where is she? Sure, she has a cell phone. I would call it frantically. "Liz, it's Mom, where are you? Please call me!"

I could never go to bed until she was home safe in hers. Her father, on the other hand, slept like a baby and left the burden of worry to me. I dozed on the couch with only the television to keep me company. I would lie there night after night crying out to God, please just bring her home safe and sound. Don't let her get hurt or in a car accident. I would listen intently for the sound of a car door slamming and the sound of the garage door as she opened it. Oh, thank you God, she's here. A flood of relief would surge through my body.

The door to the kitchen would open slowly and quietly, and she would come bounding down the stairs to the family room. "I'm home Mom," she would say.

"Where have you been, Liz – I have been worried sick!" I would exclaim, trying not to show my anger.

"Oh, I was at a party – Mom, you just worry way too much. I'm fine . . . nothing's ever going to happen to me," she would always say.

I wanted to scream – can't you see what you're doing to me? But I didn't; angry words exchanged with a teenager at 2:00 a.m. wouldn't solve anything, I told myself. She might not come home at all if she knows how angry I really am.

So, the thought of 21 days of not wondering every night about her whereabouts and safety seemed like a giant vacation on that sunny summer day. We were carefree and happy. Liz was going to have the time of her life, and so were we.

Three weeks passed quickly, though. In the blink of an eye, it was over and she was coming home. I did miss her and was very anxious to hear about her trip. As I headed home from work that day I wondered, had this been the trip she had hoped for? Had it changed her in any way?

I entered the kitchen to find Liz with her suitcases lying open on the dining room floor, and her collection of souvenirs and gifts sprawled out on the dining room table.

She looked so tired and pale – jet lag, I assumed. We hugged and she seemed genuinely happy to be home. "I had a great time, Mom," she said, and we heard all of the details of what seemed to be the best three weeks of her life. "But, I'm so tired, all I want to do is go to bed." That seemed like a reasonable request for someone who had traveled so far in just a day.

The next day, however, things were decidedly different. Liz was violently ill. A visit to the doctor confirmed it – she had mono and salmonella poisoning. Complete bed rest for at least 3-4 weeks. She slept each day for about 20 hours, only waking to eat something, maybe take a shower if she had the energy, and go to the bathroom.

As a surprise for her return, I had done a complete makeover of her bedroom. New paint on the walls, new carpeting and a new bedspread and sheets awaited her. I was happy the timing had been so perfect, as she now spent her entire summer in that room. No more late nights or wild parties, just rest, rest and more rest. Life was good.

"There's a really interesting new TV program you should watch," my sister Sue told me. It's this guy named John Edward who says he can communicate with people who have died.

Wow, I thought, it would be amazing to actually be able to communicate with the dead. I have always been fascinated with things of the spirit. I remembered my excitement in the 70s when Raymond Moody published the book, *Life After Life*. It was his investigation of the near-death experiences of many different people. I remembered reading it over and over again. It was so comforting, and I longed to have an experience like that.

So I tuned in that night. *Crossing Over* was the name of the program. And, it was just as my sister had said. This guy had a room full of people and was giving out messages from deceased loved ones. Each message seemed to make total sense to the person receiving it. It was amazing. I was hooked and I watched it every night. If I ever lost someone close to me, I thought, I sure would want to be on that show. But, how would I ever get an audience with John Edward?

I took advantage of Liz's stay-at-home condition. "Liz, I would say, come and watch *Crossing Over* with me. It is fascinating!" She watched it once and that was all. I couldn't convince her. To this day I don't know if she didn't believe in it, or if, as a 17-year-old, death held no interest to her. After all, nothing was going to happen to her. She was invincible. However, she now knew that her mother was a believer.

Summer faded into fall and Liz's senior year. She had given up cheerleading in order to spend more time with her friends during her final high school year. Her smoking, drinking and partying continued. It truly was the "year from hell" for Roger and me. But, she graduated and was accepted at the University of Minnesota in the College of Liberal Arts, which was her goal.

On August 24, 2002 we packed up her belongings and drove her to Bailey Hall on the St. Paul campus of the U of M. We unloaded her stuff, met her roommate and her parents, kissed her good-bye, and left.

Once again, it felt like a huge burden had been lifted from our shoulders. Whatever her nightly escapades would be now, we wouldn't have to know about them; any blame would be placed directly on her shoulders and not on us, her parents. Life, once again, was good.

It was as if our entire house breathed a huge sigh of relief . . . Liz was gone. The new dynamic was wonderful. Our other daughter, Anna, was the complete opposite of Liz. She was quiet, she had friends that neither smoked, drank, nor swore. She came home when she said she would. Anna was spiritual. She had a quiet, determined faith. She thought Liz was stupid for all of the things she had put us through. We trusted Anna and we no longer had to hide anything. We relaxed and started to focus on our lives again instead of on wondering what Liz would do next.

School seemed to be going very well for Liz. She was getting good grades; she got along with her roommate. She was living in an exciting metropolitan area and she had a large group of very diverse friends – all goals she had set for herself.

Roger and I decided to plan a family vacation around Liz's spring break. We searched for someplace warm, fun, and affordable. On March 15, 2003 the four of us boarded a plane for San Diego, California.

It was the best week of our lives as a family. We saw the sights, ate out at fun restaurants, went to the beach, and got along famously. The week flew by and we all commented on how much fun we had. There had not been one fight or cross word between any of us the entire week. It was a week that will burn forever bright in each of our memories. It was truly our shining hour as a family.

Liz finished her first college year and moved home for the summer. She now realized she had to work hard and make as much money as she could. She got her old job back at the restaurant and got plenty of hours. She worked very hard all summer and earned an impressive amount of money for school. She even landed herself a part-time job for the school year at a jewelry store at the Mall of America, because she was a good waitress and very personable, and happened to wait on the jewelry store owners. They engaged her in conversation, asking what her plans were and did she need a part-time job for school? She was thrilled.

Every year since the girls were in kindergarten, I would always take them school shopping. This year would be no exception. Teenagers don't typically want to spend time with their parents. But girls do love to shop, so that was my way of spending time with them. I hated to shop, but the joy of spending the day with the two of them, and seeing the excitement and happiness on each of their faces, more than made up for my dislike of large malls or my large credit card bill.

This year, however, my job was on the line. The customer service position I held was sure to be outsourced to a company in Pennsylvania. "You'd better enjoy this, girls," I told them several times that day. "This may be the last time we ever get to do this." Little did I know just how prophetic those words would be. In retrospect, I think of that day often. Did I subconsciously know the real reason why the three of us would never again shop together?

We moved Liz into her off-campus house on September 1, 2003. It was a bright and sunny Labor Day. We pulled out of town with her grandpa's pickup loaded to the gills with every possession she could cram in.

Despite my early fears, the house was fine. It was old, but it was clean. Liz was sharing a bedroom with her friend, Amanda. Also living in the house were Monique, her roommate from last year, and two girls I didn't know well, Bri and Afton. Two guys rounded out the group, Brian and Fik. I was actually happy to have the guys there. Extra protection for my girl, I thought. I watched as they were all reunited after a summer apart. They hugged each other and were so genuinely happy to be together again. It reminded me of the TV Show *Friends*. They were their own little family, so excited to be starting this new chapter in their lives.

It was hot as we lugged Liz's mattress up the stairs. Fans were strategically placed to cool us as much as possible. We put the bed frame together and the mattress and box spring were in place. I volunteered to make the bed, so she and her dad could start to bring in her clothes.

It was a sunny room with a large double window right next to her bed. As I finished with the sheets and bedspread, I pushed the bed up against the wall and gazed out the window. I distinctly remember thinking to myself . . . if anything ever happens, she can always jump out the window.

Roger and I headed south towards home, breathing yet another sigh of relief. In all probability, Liz would be living there the rest of her college years. No more summers at home. We even had a drink that night to toast our newfound freedom.

Liz's 20th birthday was Friday, September 12th. We had already given her several gifts before she left – new lamps for her living room and a large box of kitchen utensils.

But, we still made plans to come up on Saturday, September 13th to take her and Monique to lunch. As I prepared to leave work that Friday afternoon, my phone rang. I had won four tickets to the Minnesota Wild Hockey game on Friday, September 19th.

Roger and I had made plans to go up north fishing that weekend with my parents. I knew we couldn't use the tickets. So I planned to give them to Liz. With two guys living in the house, they were sure to be a hit. I purposely did not tell Liz that we were going up north. She didn't need to know, I told myself. I did not want to take the chance that she would decide to come home and have a wild party. No, we would go up north and we would be home by the weekend, and she would never know the difference.

We had a great lunch that Saturday afternoon. As it turned out, Monique was ill and couldn't join us. So we brought Amanda. We didn't know her very well so it was a chance to get acquainted. We went to Old Chicago and talked and laughed. We gave Liz a card with the tickets. She was thrilled. Who would she take, she considered. Well, Manda, she said, you get first dibbs because you are the first to know about them. "I'll definitely go," she said. "And, I have to take Fik and Brian. They'd never forgive me," Liz said. So it was settled. The four of them would make a night of it.

Liz had decided she wanted her extended family to come to her house on Saturday, September 27th, to see her new place and celebrate her birthday and that of her Uncle Randy and Aunt Barb. We all made plans to eat at the Olive Garden Restaurant and then we would all go to Liz's for cake and to open presents.

When we dropped her off, I reminded her of our upcoming visit. The house was a mess. An empty beer keg stood in the porch and dirty dishes were all over the kitchen. "The house had better not look like this when Grandma comes, Liz." "Oh, it won't, Mom. I promise it will be clean." With that, I kissed her cheek, gave her another hug, and wished her a final Happy Birthday. After all, it would only be a couple of weeks and we would see her again.

The following Wednesday at about ten minutes to five our phone rang, and it was Liz. She was frantic. She was due at her new job at 5:00 p.m. and couldn't find the Mall of America. She was on 494 going west. "Liz, calm down and take the next exit," I told her. You need to be on 494 East. "Look for the Cedar Avenue exit." "Will you stay on the phone with me until I find it?" "Of course, I will." She calmed down and looked for the exit. "I don't see Cedar but there's 77?" "That's it," I exclaimed. She took the exit and soon saw signs to the Mall. "I'm okay now, thanks, Mom." "You're welcome sweetie," I told her. "Have a great night."

About 9:00 p.m. I started to think of her, as I knew her shift would be over. Would she remember how to retrace her steps to get back home? I called her cell phone and got her voice mail. "Liz, if you need help getting back home, give me a call, okay?" Ten minutes later she called. I'm fine, Mom. I'm almost at the University exit. My job was sooo much fun, Mom, and the people are so nice. I love it." I was so pleased. I told her I loved her and we hung up. Little did I know that would be the last conversation I would ever have with my daughter.

The next day, Roger and I, along with my parents, headed up north for a four-day fishing trip. We arrived on Thursday afternoon and fished a little that day and nearly all day on Friday. On Saturday, we decided the guys would go out for some early morning fishing and Mom and I would stay back. The guys promised to return by 9:00 a.m. for breakfast. It was a leisurely morning. We made coffee and relaxed. We had the TV on the one and only station that came in. It was 8:00 a.m. and the Saturday morning news had just started. "I'm going to take a shower," my mom said. I relaxed and poured myself another cup of coffee. I was reading and only half listening to the news.

I decided to start the early preparations for a big Saturday morning breakfast. With the bacon just starting to softly sizzle, I continued to drink coffee and get caught up with my magazine reading. I heard the newscaster report an early morning fire in southeast Minneapolis. It was a duplex housing University of Minnesota students. That caught my ear. Liz lived in southeast Minneapolis, her house was a duplex . . . but, I figured, there are many duplexes in southeast Minneapolis for U of M students.

Mom was now out of the shower and I could hear the hum of the hair dryer. The news was about over. Suddenly, they broke in with an update on the fire. One dead, they reported. Then they gave the address. My heart felt like it had just stopped beating and I was going to be sick. 827 SE 15th Street, oh my God . . . I think that's Liz's address. If it isn't, it's really close.

Mom was done in the bathroom and she came out to the kitchen to check on the progress I was making with breakfast. "Mom, I think there's been a fire at Liz's house! They just said the address, and I think it's hers."

"Oh, my God, are you sure" she said, with concern in her eyes. "Where are the guys? They should be here by now."

We both felt the rise of panic in our stomachs, but I think we were each trying to remain calm for the other.

We walked down to the dock, craning our necks trying to see an incoming boat, or to hear the faint sound of a motor. "Where are they?" we cried. Finally, after about ten minutes, we heard the faint sound of a boat motor and saw a small speck of a boat getting larger . . . here they come. They were not even at the dock yet and I was yelling to Roger, "What is Liz's address?"

They both looked puzzled seeing us standing there, sensing the terror in our faces.

"I think there's been a fire at Liz's house," I said. "Do you remember her address?"

"I think it's 16th Street SE," Roger said.

"Are you sure?"

"No, but I have it written down in my wallet."

We ran back to the cabin. Roger rummaged around for his billfold. He found it, opened it, and pulled out a small slip of paper. "827 15th Street SE," he said. He had read the exact address that was on the news just minutes ago.

"Oh God, it is her house."

The guys went to the lodge to call for information. Mom and I decided to wait in the cabin. The minutes ticked by. "I can't stand it, I have to know," I told Mom. We headed over to the lodge.

We walked in and my dad was on the phone. In the span of about five minutes we went from one dead to three dead – two girls, one guy. No, No, No. This cannot be happening. "What color is her hair? What color are her eyes? Does she have any tattoos?"

Those horrible, disgusting tattoos – even though they were small and inconspicuous, I had always hated them, and now they were the very things that confirmed our deepest fear. And, I'll never forget the look on my dad's face . . . his color was gone. Okay, he said and hung up the phone. "It doesn't look good," was all he said to us. He didn't have to say the words – we all knew. "We have to leave," we told the resort owners.

We walked back to the cabin and began the arduous task of packing up. We were all strangely calm. No one went crazy like we all wanted to. We knew we had to concentrate on the task at hand. We packed in record time and headed out.

It was the longest five hours of my life. But, in thinking back, the time was helpful. We had five hours where we could just sit. We didn't have to talk. We could all try to come to terms with what we knew we were going to face when we got home. But still, we all held out that little bit of hope that maybe, just maybe, it wasn't her. It was just a huge, terrible mistake. Not our Liz. Please God, not our Liz.

"Drive to the house," I told Roger. I have to see it. I won't believe it until I see it. I could feel my heart beating a million times a minute. We parked our car a block away in a little park that had room for us. I got out and ran to the house. I came up from the back. I could see the burned out windows on the second floor.

I ran through the gate and along the path on the side of the house. I saw a group of people standing there. I saw Bri and her mother. Bri's back was towards me and she didn't see me, but her mother did, and she said, "Oh my God."

"Is it Liz," I cried?

"Yes," she said.   "It's Liz, Brian and Amanda."

Oh God, now it's real.

I just stood there; I was strangely calm and I didn't know why. Suddenly I was hit from behind. It was Monique, Liz's closest college friend. She was sobbing uncontrollably and was inconsolable. I tried to comfort her, but I could not. We walked around in a daze. Friends were there and a policeman was on guard to keep us out of the house. We tried to comfort the kids. They were devastated. Their friends were dead and their house and all its belongings were gone.

With nothing more that could be done, we headed south. We were stunned. It was now a reality.   Our girl, our first-born daughter and granddaughter, was dead.

When   we   arrived   home   our   focus immediately became our other daughter, Anna. She was at a church retreat in Iowa. I didn't have the name of the church or the phone number. We tried to reach the on-call minister at our church but only got her voicemail.

With no other choice, we drove to our church. There was a Saturday night service going on. We tried to find someone who could give us the information that we needed.

Finding no one other than the 200 or so worshippers who were intently listening to the sermon, Roger walked up the side aisle and motioned to the minister who was not giving the sermon. Quietly, Roger whispered that we needed to reach Anna but didn't have the retreat information. He told Roger the number was on his desk in his office. We found it and headed back home.

Roger called the retreat center and was able to reach our Junior High Youth Director, Jess. In a calm and matter-of-fact manner he told her that Liz was dead, and we needed to pick up Anna. I could hear her scream into the phone as the reality of it hit her. After all, Jess knew Liz well. I don't have many regrets, but this is one I do have. I just wish I could have been the one to break it to her. We put tremendous pressure on her, as we decided that the 2-1/2 hour trip to pick up Anna was more than we could handle that day. We made the decision to let her finish out the retreat and return with the group the following day. After all, there was nothing she could do and the longer we could keep the horrible news from her, the better.

However, Jess now had to keep this in confidence, as we wanted to be the ones to tell Anna. How very very difficult that must have been for her. Jess was devastated; and now, she had to carry on as if nothing was wrong.

We turned on the news and it was the leading story. To our horror, the names of the dead had been released to the media. We hadn't even thought about the rest of our family. Hurriedly, Roger drove to his mother's apartment and broke the news to her. We weren't as fortunate with Roger's sisters. They had to learn the news from the radio. They came over to be with us.

It was now totally crazy. The phone was ringing off the hook. The media wanted to talk to us. They came to our doorstep and rang our doorbell. Could we talk to them? They just wanted to know how we felt. How do we feel? Do they really know what they are saying? How do you think we feel? Our daughter is dead. What do you want us to say? Needless to say, we turned them away. The media did as they always do, trying to make a story bigger. Quick to place blame, they brought out the past history of the landlords and the many housing violations they had. Right away, I felt this was wrong. I didn't think the landlords were at fault. Couldn't they at least wait a few days until the investigation was complete before making these insinuations?

By 11:00 p.m. everyone had gone home. We turned off the phone and turned out the porch light. It was just Roger and me. How do you sleep when your daughter has died? I sure didn't. I lay stone cold awake the entire night. My mind would not turn off. I don't remember what my thoughts were, but I never slept. About 6:00 a.m. I got up, made a pot of coffee and walked outside and brought in the Sunday paper.

I opened it up and there on the front page was the fire story with Liz's picture next to it. It wasn't a nightmare, I told myself. It was real, and I couldn't believe it. The picture of her next to the story brought me to my knees on the kitchen floor.

As I lifted up my head and cried out, my eyes became fixed on our answering machine. The light was blinking, signaling messages. I pushed the button and suddenly I heard Liz's voice through throngs of people. "Hi Mom, it's Liz. I'm at the game and I wanted to thank you for those tickets. They're really awesome seats, so thank you very much. Bye."

Oh my God, I can hardly believe my ears – a final message from my girl. Those tickets I gave her for the Wild hockey game – I had forgotten. She didn't know we weren't at home and she called us. A final gift . . . a gift that we will save forever. We have it recorded on our computer and it plays occasionally as I listen to music and play my daily game of spider solitaire. We will always have the sound of our daughter's voice. What a precious gift.

I considered it a miracle. Just one of many, I would soon learn.

It was 10:30 a.m. and we had to go make the arrangements for the funeral. We walked in the door of the funeral home and it was eerily quiet. It was so difficult to be in this place of death knowing that somewhere in the building lay my daughter's lifeless body. We pulled ourselves together and did what had to be done.

Burial clothes . . . she needed clothes . . . but she took them all with her when she moved into that house. How ironic is this? The girl I just took shopping three weeks ago, now had nothing to wear. I had to laugh at the absurdity of it all. "Well, Liz," I told her, "you're going to get yourself another new outfit." I had absolutely no idea of what to purchase as my sister and I headed out to the mall. "Liz," I said, "I need your help."

In a relatively short amount of time, I picked out a pair of khaki pants and a light blue sweater. I thought it would be okay. Would Liz approve? I didn't know. But did it really matter?

A few weeks later Roger's sister told me she had been going through some pictures and found one of Liz taken at our Christmas gathering the year before. She was wearing a pair of khaki pants and a light blue sweater. That made me smile.

My cell phone rang. It was Jess, our Youth Director. The bus was ten minutes from arriving at our church. Roger and I were going to meet it and tell Anna. "I'll go in right away and open up an office so you can take Anna in and talk to her," Jess told us.

We reached the church before the bus did, and we sat in the car and waited. How could we break this to Anna? There would be no good way to do it. The bus pulled in. We got out and leaned against the car as we waited to see her. She was one of the first off. She saw us and started to walk towards us with a quizzical look on her face. "Are you supposed to be here," she said?

"No," we said, "but we are."

Immediately she knew something was wrong. "Tell me please – just tell me," she screamed.

"We will, but let's go into the church first," we said.

We walked her into the building, and she was still screaming, "Just tell me, just tell me."

I think she thought it would be bad news about one of her grandparents. We stepped into the small office and sat her down on a couch. I took a huge deep breath. "Honey, there's been a fire at Liz's house."

"Oh, no," she shrieked.

"I know, honey, I know. Liz is gone, honey. She's dead."

Anna screamed and cried. "No, no. Not Liz."

"Yes, honey."

We let her cry for as long as she needed to. Then we had to leave the office, collect her belongings and drive home.

Jess was there to give us each a hug and offer her support. Anna's friends looked confused. "Anna's sister died yesterday," I told them. They huddled around us for support as well.

We collected Anna's stuff and got her in the car. We drove her home. Anna got out and we helped her into the house. When she opened the door she was greeted by a myriad of people who had come to our house to be with us. Anna wasn't ready to deal with any of them. She went to her room to be alone with her thoughts. She spent about fifteen minutes by herself. We sent Maddy in to check on her. She was okay. She came out of her room and accepted the hugs and sympathy that our friends and family had come to offer.

The day of the visitation was here. It was the day I dreaded the most. Today I would have to see my daughter in a casket. I asked God to help me get through this day. He did.

The visitation started at 4:00 p.m. but Roger, Anna and I went at 2:00 p.m.. We had pictures to set up, and we wanted it to be just the three of us when we saw Liz for the first time. I asked the funeral director to please have the casket closed until we were ready. We brought in many pictures. The boards we had put together for her graduation now had a new purpose. We found the Faith paper she had written for confirmation. Also found were poems and stories she had written about her closest friends; and the scrapbooks she had put together that summer showing all her cheerleading accomplishments. All so precious now, and each gave a good sense of who my girl was for those who didn't know her.

We had everything set up the way we wanted it. The dreaded time was here. The funeral director gently opened the lid and we stepped forward. The next twenty minutes were a total blur. There was my girl. She looked beautiful. Only a small bruise on the bridge of her nose gave a clue to the trauma her body had undergone.

It was as though time stood still. I began to cry as I have never cried before. It was a deep guttural cry that came from deep within my soul. Sounds were coming out of my mouth that I had absolutely no control over. We all three cried the same deep cries of complete anguish. I stroked Liz's hair and I touched her hands. She was as hard as a rock. That sounds harsh, but it made me realize that she wasn't in this body anymore. It was just a remnant of her previous life. As quickly as my anguished cries began, they ceased. It was as though someone had flipped a switch and I was done. I can't explain it. I've never cried like that before or since.

The outpouring of love and support that we received that day was absolutely unbelievable. If half this number shows up when I die, I would be happy, I thought. People were lined up continuously from 4:00 p.m. until 9:30 p.m. What a wonderful tribute for a girl who was only on the earth for a short 20 years.

It was very hard on Liz's friends. They could no longer hold on to the fallacy that they were invincible. Liz had proven to them that they were not. And seeing her in that casket made them come to terms with the cruel turns life can take. It was a hard lesson that had to be learned.

One of Liz's closest friends, Cassie, came through the line. She hugged me and with tears in her eyes, she whispered to me. "I just want you to know, Liz has come to me and let me know that she is okay." "Oh, Cassie. Thank you for telling me," I said, and I hugged her again. Wow, I wanted to hear more about that, but now was not the time. I filed it away to be dealt with later.

We left the funeral home about 10:30 p.m. that night. It was the most bizarre thing. I had absolutely no attachment to that body lying in the casket. It was just there; my girl was not in it. She had gone on to bigger and better things. We walked out the door and didn't look back.

The next day at the funeral we kept the casket closed, to the dismay of some of the relatives who weren't able to attend the visitation. "I'm sorry," I said. "But, it's just too difficult." I didn't want to risk a horrible scene at the casket when it was time to close it.

Close family members and Liz's friends all gathered in the church lounge for a prayer before the service began. My niece, Maddy, who was an accomplished piano player, asked to play a song for Liz, which she did so beautifully at the very beginning of the service. We were all lined up in the back of the church waiting for the processional to begin. Maddy finished her song and walked back to be with us. Wow, I thought, the church is full and they are starting to set up folding chairs. The music began and we walked up. It was a surreal feeling and I don't remember much of it. Flowers were everywhere – up on the chancel and all around the casket.

Four people asked to speak at the funeral. First was Monique, who spoke of how she had grown to love Liz and all her quirks. She told of how she had to "iron" Liz's hair. And, how Liz hated certain words like "daiquiri" and "moist." And, how they had made plans to move to California after graduation and open a shop and sell incense, candles, limes, and dill pickle chips --- favorites of each. Next came Kelly, Liz's older cousin. Then Anni and Beth, close high school friends. Even though it was a funeral, laughter rippled through the crowd at times, as we all shared funny memories of our Liz.

It was a beautiful day as the service ended and we all lined up in our cars to head to the cemetery. The drive was fraught with memories as the processional passed by the high school, then by our house and then her grandpa and grandma's house just one more time.

My mom wanted to release butterflies at the cemetery. It was a good idea, but no one knew where to find them. Not even the florist. But, my mom would not be deterred. She went on the Internet, found a company in California that supplied butterflies, ordered them, and had them delivered in time for the funeral – quite a feat for a grandmother who on a good day can barely remember how to open up her email.

The next day Anna went back to school and Roger and I went to White Bear Lake to attend Amanda's funeral. That morning before we left, the doorbell rang and it was Cassie. The restaurant where Liz worked had sent us some of her favorite food, shrimp pasta, and Cassie got to deliver it. It tasted especially good. Now was my chance.

"Cassie," I said, "tell me what happened when you got that message from Liz."

"I can't explain it," she said. "I was driving around in my car thinking of all the memories I had with her and all of a sudden she was just there. I couldn't see her, but I felt her presence so strongly and she said, 'Cassie, I'm okay, you don't have to worry about me.'"

That's wonderful . . . amazing, I thought to myself.

A couple of days later Liz sent another message. This time my mom was the lucky recipient. The cemetery is almost in my parents' backyard, it is so close; so they go there often. A day after the funeral, Mom was there. As she stared at the overturned earth and the flowers that lay strewn upon it, she thought to herself, "Liz, if you're okay, please give me a sign." After a few more minutes of contemplation, she turned and started to walk back home. Suddenly, seemingly out of nowhere, two monarch butterflies rose up and flew in front of her. That was my mom's sign. A grieving grandmother sees butterflies – a living symbol of rebirth and new life. Liz is indeed alive, and she was making her presence known. Knowing this brought me such peace and happiness.

Saturday, September 27th, the fire investigation was complete. Just as I had thought, the landlords were not at fault. The fire was ruled accidental, but the exact cause was not known. The crime tape was down and the families and surviving roommates were allowed back in the house to claim any belongings that could be salvaged. Roger, my dad and Anna headed up to the house. We wanted to find Liz's purse, with her billfold and driver's license and whatever else could be salvaged. There was no electricity, so their efforts were hampered by darkness as well as the thick wet insulation that coated the upstairs bedrooms. Still, they were successful in locating her purse. They also brought home a charcoal portrait she had done of herself in France, a lot of her jewelry, her bed frame, some knick-knacks, and a sweater.

Roger made a second trip to the house by himself. Brian's parents wanted his dresser but had no room to bring it home. Roger retrieved it and brought it our house to store until they could come and pick it up. He was on his way home, alone in the jeep with only the highway and his thoughts to keep him company. "Well," he thought to himself, "I'm bringing her stuff home, but I sure wish I was bringing her home." Suddenly, he heard his daughter's voice loud and crystal clear. "I'm already home, Dad," she said. Sign number three. Another miracle. Roger acknowledged it as a sign and actually told me. I considered that a miracle as well.

Wow, three signs from my girl – all within a week of her death – each totally different, but yet so appropriate for each person. I loved it. I thought, I'm not ready yet, Liz, but when I am, I'll let you know.

I didn't have to ask and I didn't have to wait very long. October 20th was here, the one-month anniversary. I was so distraught I didn't go to work that day.

Instead, I stayed home and read through all the cards we had received, and finished up some thank-you notes, in between having a few good cries. Anna came home from school and Roger came home from work. We had supper and I cleaned up the kitchen. Roger and Anna were doing something on the computer.

As I put the last of the dishes in the cupboard, the smoke alarm went off. It was blaring. Oh my gosh! I ran downstairs, through the family room – nothing; Anna's room – nothing; Liz's room – nothing. Still the alarm continued to blare, but I couldn't tell where it was coming from. I ran frantically back upstairs through the kitchen, the dining room, the living room, and down the hall to the bedrooms. There was no smoke or sign of a fire anywhere. I stopped short in the hall when it suddenly quit. Well, that was weird, I thought to myself. Our alarms have never gone off like that before. Then I heard Roger and Anna talking in the computer room as if nothing had happened. Then it dawned on me – they didn't hear the alarms. Hmm . . .

Oh, my God . . . the one-month anniversary and a smoke alarm? It made perfect sense. It was Liz! She had given me a sign and I got it! And, I didn't even have to ask. Wow, wow wow! This was amazing!

Okay, I think with my sensible mind, I bet this means she's going to give me a sign on the 20th of every month. That seemed totally logical. So a week before November 20th, I started to ask her.

Okay, Liz, I'm ready for a sign on November 20th. I told her that every day for a week. Only November 20th came and went and nothing happened. Well, I guess that theory goes out the window, I told myself.

The next day was Friday, November 21st, just a typical day. It was a few minutes past 10:00 p.m., and I was in my usual spot – sprawled out on the couch and asleep, pretty much my nightly ritual. However, for some reason, I woke up, grabbed the TV remote, and changed the channel – all done very mechanically and without any thought. The news was on and they were showing scenes for an upcoming story. They showed a cemetery and they zoomed in on a gravesite. There was a wind chime there that was identical to the one we had at Liz's grave at the time. I was now fully awake and began to wonder what the story would be. It definitely had my attention, and I knew it was crucial that I watched it.

The story was about a woman who lived in the Minneapolis area who can communicate with people who have died. I could hardly believe it.

They showed her in a room with four other people and she was able to go to each one and tell them about their loved one. I was stunned and totally dumbfounded. Thoughts of John Edward immediately went through my mind.

The next morning I went on the website of the television station to try to view the story again just to be sure it really happened. I didn't even know the name of the woman in the story. I wasn't very successful. But I did happen upon the email address of the reporter who did the story. I carefully composed an email and sent it to her. I told her who I was and that my daughter was one of the U of M students who died in that house fire a couple of months ago. I had seen her story about the woman who speaks to the dead and did she know if this woman did this for ordinary people? If so, did she know how I could contact her?

My email was only a few hours old when I checked for a reply, and I had one. My heart leapt with anticipation. Her name is Kathryn Harwig, Randi told me. I'm sure she would see you. She gave me Kathryn's personal email address and told me to tell Kathryn that she had sent me. As it turned out, Randi had actually gone to her for a session to deal with her own father's death. She had firsthand knowledge. It was amazing, she said. It had helped her tremendously and she was a different person because of it. Randi was so nice and very encouraging. She even told me I could call her if I needed to talk.

It took me a couple of days to get up the courage to email Kathryn. But I did. I was careful not to give her much information. I had lost someone very close to me, I said. Did she do readings for people? Kathryn answered me quickly as well. She was sorry for my loss and she had a website with all of her pertinent information. Yes, she did readings for people. Even though I was at work and shouldn't have been going to indiscriminant websites, I couldn't help myself. I went to her website, www.harwig.com, and the first thing that came up was her biography. I started to read it and I could barely contain myself.

Her college majors were Psychology and Sociology – the same as Liz's. She had gone to the

University of Minnesota for her master's in criminal justice and she worked for many years as a probation officer with dangerous criminals. Liz's career goal was to become a Criminal Psychologist and work with dangerous criminals. I could never understand her desire to do that kind of work, but it had been her goal for a number of years. Liz's favorite movie was, you guessed it, *Silence of the Lambs*. I was totally stunned. The similarities between Liz and Kathryn were overwhelming, and I took this as a huge sign that my daughter was in on this and would come through for me. Why, Kathryn even drove a Saturn. I laughed uncontrollably when I read that. We had a Saturn for 9 years. It was to become Liz's car, until she had an accident and totaled it back on the 4th of July.

I don't like to drive, especially in metro areas. It had been a fear that I had yet to get over, even at the ripe old age of 49. Who could I get to drive me to this reading? I knew who it wouldn't be. I tried to tell Roger about this, assuming that since I had been open to hearing about his sign from Liz, that he would be happy to hear mine. Wrong. I barely got started when he raised his hand and said, "I don't want to hear any more. She just wants to take your money." What a disappointment. But I was undeterred. I thought of my sister Sue. She would be receptive to this. After all, she was the one who had told me about John Edward. Thanksgiving was just a few days away. I'll tell her then, I thought, and maybe we can even schedule an appointment over her Christmas break.

Thanksgiving Day came, but there was never a good time to pull Sue aside and tell her my news. I had the long weekend so I wasn't too worried. We went on our usual day-after-Thanksgiving shopping trip and had a good time. But the timing still just wasn't right.

On Saturday morning the phone rang. It was my niece, Maddy. "Kim, I'm calling to tell you that Grandpa's in the hospital. They think he may have had a heart attack." Oh God, no. I screamed and threw down the phone and quickly drove to the hospital. Not my dad, too – you can't do this, God. Please God. Please.

I got to the hospital and Dad was in the ER. They were running an EKG. It revealed a mild heart attack. But, he was stable and they gave him something for the pain. We all calmed down. He stayed in the hospital for a couple of days. They said he could go home if he passed a stress test on Monday. But he flunked it, big time. Roger called me at work. Dad was going to the Mayo Clinic to be evaluated for heart surgery. Did I want to ride along with Mom? Of course. We drove over and found Dad's room. He was busy answering many questions from a myriad of different doctors. They would do an angiogram tomorrow and that would tell them what needed to be done.

The angiogram showed multiple blockages. Dad was scheduled for bypass surgery the next day. He was in the best possible hospital for this kind of surgery. I was concerned, but not overly worried. Dad came through the surgery with flying colors. They opened up five blockages. Thank you, God. You spared my dad. He could have died, but he didn't.

Needless to say, telling Sue about going to see a medium was the farthest thing from my mind. The next few weeks were focused on Dad and making sure he was okay.

Christmas rolled around and it was tough – our first without Liz. We kept our traditions the same. It seemed like the best thing to do. After all, we had Anna, Maddy and Thomas to think of. They deserved a good Christmas. And I knew it was what Liz would have wanted.

Sue was home for a couple of weeks – being a teacher has its perks, and long holiday vacations are one of them. I got up my nerve and told her that Liz had given me a sign. I told her about the smoke alarm and Kathryn.

"Will you go with me, Sue?" I asked.

"Yes," she said, "but I can't go until school is done in June."

"Not a problem," I said. "I can wait."

Sue went back home, and the first Sunday in January we invited Liz's high school friends to our house for supper before they all headed back to their respective colleges. I so loved it when "the girls," as they call themselves, came over. They loved to be in the house. "There are so many memories here," they said. Liz loved to have her friends spend the night. Each of them had spent many a night next to Liz or in a sleeping bag on her bedroom floor. We all ended up in Liz's room and the girls would look through her closets and her drawers. They all had at least one piece of her clothing. She was famous for giving away clothes she didn't want anymore, or absentmindedly leaving them behind at someone's house.

"Whatever you have, keep it, girls," I said. "Wear it and remember our Lizzie." Whenever "the girls" were in the house, I seemed to feel Liz's presence. That night, the air felt electric and her essence permeated my very being. I was on a high.

I still felt it the next day. I went to work and could not concentrate on anything except the strong feeling of her presence the night before, and the constant thought of making an appointment to see Kathryn. I lost count of the times I pulled her website up on my computer and read it over and over again; or, the countless times I would read and re-read the email she had sent me.

It took me until mid-afternoon that day to realize that I couldn't wait until June. I had to go now. But whom could I get to drive me?

Suddenly I thought of my friend Julie. I had told her about my sign and of this Intuitive named Kathryn. She drives in the cities. She was open. She had told me about some things that had happened to her that she felt had come from her parents who had recently passed. I got up my nerve and the next day I said, "Hey Julie, how would you like to go on a road trip to Maple Grove?" She knew right away what I meant and quickly agreed.

That settled it. I had someone to drive me. Oh, God, now I just have to get up the courage to call Kathryn. I was a wreck. Once again, not much work was done at my job that day. I've got to call her and get it over with, I told myself, so I can quit thinking about this and do my job.

I dialed her number and it rang a few times and went to her answering machine. I breathed a huge sigh of relief and left my name and number and told her I would like to make an appointment.

I went to lunch and when I returned the light on my phone was blinking. I had a message. Could it be Kathryn? It was. I called her back. I could barely talk, I was so nervous. She couldn't have been nicer. Her voice was so soft and soothing. I felt like she really cared about me. We set the date. January 16th at 2:00 p.m. – a mere ten days away. She gave me directions to her studio, and said she'd see me soon. I hung up the phone, and I was exhausted. I'd done it. But how would I ever get through these next ten days?

I did, but not without questioning my sanity on a daily basis. Who did I think I was kidding? How could I possibly think that I could talk to Liz? She was dead. It's just not possible, I told myself. But, what if it is possible? I had to find out. I sent an email to Randi, the TV reporter who had been so nice to me. Randi, I said, I'm a wreck. I've made my appointment with Kathryn, but what if I get there and nothing happens? Then it will just be a big mistake and I'll have to admit that it was just the fantasy of a grieving mother. Did she have any doubts before she went to her session?

Just as before, Randi quickly responded. "What you are feeling is totally normal," she told me. I was so concerned my dad wouldn't be there, but he arrived before I did. And it was amazing." She told me to talk to Liz and ask her to please come. "Do it everyday," she said. "Kathryn says spirits love to help, but they need to be asked."

Okay, that's not hard; I can do that. And, I did. In fact, I did it many times a day. I did it so much I could almost hear Liz saying, "Okay already, will you quit bugging me! You know I'll be there!"

Randi sent me an email saying, "I'll be thinking of you on the 16th, and I'd love to hear how it went if you want to talk." Wow. I'm sending and receiving emails from someone I watched on TV every night. How cool is that?

Finally the day arrived. There was nothing to stop us. The weather was fine for traveling. We arrived at Kathryn's studio. I had to force myself to get out of the car. My legs felt like dead weights. But, I'd come too far to turn back now. We walked up the steps and rang the bell. The door opened and there she was. She welcomed us into her beautiful studio. A large window brought lots of light into a very white, beautiful room. I sat down on her large comfortable couch, took a deep breath, and all my anxieties just seemed to fade away. Kathryn took my hand, studied it and started to talk.

"Your parents are coming through and they don't approve." Well, that was for sure. I hadn't even thought of telling them, as I knew they would not.

"Then there's a man. This isn't anyone you would know. He says he's your guide and he wants to know if you want to take his hand and go on this journey with him."

"Yes," I said.

"And now there's a little girl, and she says she is your daughter. Do you want to talk to her?"

"Yes, that is the reason that I am here. But how old is she?"

"Well, she looks to be about 6 or 7; however, she was older when she died, about 19."

Well, I thought, that's pretty close. She was 20 for a week.

"She wants you to know that she is fine and she is happy. She wants you to know that she passed quickly and didn't have any pain." At first Kathryn thinks she died in a car accident because she sees Liz and several others in a car. No, I said, she was in a car that night, and it was an accident, but not a car accident. Kathryn thinks a little bit more and then she sees the car driving to a house and then the house explodes. Yes, that's it.

Liz was crazy – running around and skipping and hopping. "She is so happy to be in spirit," Kathryn tells me. She knew she was going down the wrong road and she didn't know how to get off. When the fire happened it was her way out. "Yes, I died but so what," she said to Kathryn. Sounds like something my wild and crazy daughter would say.

Before I knew it, the hour was up and I had run out of things to ask or say to her. Yet I didn't want it to end.

I knew with complete certainty that Kathryn was indeed talking to my girl. She captured the very essence of her personality perfectly.

I was numb as we drove home and listened again to my session on the tape recording that Kathryn gave me. I was in a fog. It took a few days for it to clear. I couldn't get over how amazing my experience had been.

Not only did I feel without a doubt that I had talked to my girl, but I couldn't get over the wonderful feeling of peace and serenity I had as I sat on that couch in Kathryn's studio. She had done thousands of readings for people, yet she knew just how important this was for me. She was amazing. But there was more to it than that. I felt connected to her for some reason that I didn't know. Maybe it was because of her wonderful gift and the fact that she was my connection to Liz. But, there was something else. She was a genuinely nice person. And, we aren't that far apart in age. I think I would like her even if she didn't have an intuitive bone in her body.

The reading I had so anticipated had come and now it was over. Now what? Do I just file this away in my memory as one of the highlights of my life? I didn't want my connection to Kathryn to end, and I would occasionally email her. She always answered me and was so nice and reassuring.

I hadn't had one dream of Liz since she died. I was puzzled by this and would occasionally ask her to please visit me in my dreams. It was what I wanted. On March 26th I got my wish, but as it turned out, it wasn't what I needed after all.

I was in our family room sitting on the floor with a game board in front of me. I looked to my left and I knew that Liz was sitting on the floor next to me. I gazed over and saw that she had on these black dress shoes that she had worn when she was about six years old. "Aren't those shoes too small for you," I asked her? She didn't answer me and I found my eyes going up her leg as far as her waist. I suddenly realized that she was wearing leggings and a sweatshirt. It was an outfit that had been her favorite when she was six. I could not get myself to look at her face. Suddenly she jumped up and started to walk into Anna's bedroom.

Oh no, I thought, she's leaving! Liz, can I have a hug? She ran back and gave me a huge hug. I started to sob. She slowly melted away and I woke up crying. I felt as though my heart had been ripped from my chest. She had been so close and now she was gone . . . again. I was sad again. That sure wasn't what I needed. I think Liz knew it, but I had been so persistent in asking that she gave it to me anyway. I had learned my lesson. I wouldn't be asking for that again.

I told no one of my visit to Kathryn for several months. I knew I would not tell Roger. I didn't know about Anna. I would tell Sue, but I wasn't sure when. Finally, about April, I broke the news to her that I had gone. It was amazing, but it was also painful, I told her. I added that I still wanted to go with her in June as we originally planned. I was beginning to think of more questions I could ask Liz, or things we could talk about.

Memorial Day was fast approaching. It was almost time for our annual trip up north for fishing, swimming and relaxing. It was something we had done for ten years. It had been so much fun. Now, it would only be Roger and me. Anna was staying home to attend some of her friend's early graduation parties. It will still be fun, I told myself; it will just be a different kind of fun.

And it was. We fished and sat by the pool and enjoyed the weather. Friday night during the middle of the night I heard Liz say to me in a loud, clear voice, "I love you, Mom!"

Oh, I love you too sweetie, I told her back in my mind. I was so relaxed I just drifted back to sleep.

I remembered it in the morning and tried to sleep as long as I could just in case she wanted to tell me something else. She didn't. But that was okay. I loved hearing her voice again. And, there is nothing better than hearing that you are loved.

Anna was graduating and I had something else to focus on. I was bound and determined that Anna's graduation party would truly be all about Anna and not about the person who was not there, Liz. We had a great party and everyone showed up to support us. It was fun. We invited "the girls" as well as Liz's roommates from college. They all came. It was wonderful.

I so hoped that the opportunity would present itself for me to tell Cassie about my visit with Kathryn. After all, she had stepped out in faith and told me about her sign from Liz. "Cassie," I said, "don't leave until I have a chance to talk to you." As she and a couple of "the girls" ended up in Liz's room, I had to join them, despite the fact that I should have been out in the garage with the rest of the party.

I told them all about Kathryn and my session, and I said I was going back soon for another visit. They were all interested and listened to me.

"Have you felt Liz's presence since the first time?" I asked.

"Yes," Cassie said, "sometimes when we are all together I can feel her. "

"Wonderful," I said.

Sue made plans to come for the 4th of July. Suddenly I had a brainstorm. I had Monday, July 5th off from work. I asked Sue if I should try to get an appointment with Kathryn on that day. "Yes, that would work," she said. I emailed Kathryn. Yes, she was free on Monday, July 5th. How about 2:00 p.m.? So, it was set. My next visit was only a few short weeks away.

My list of questions grew longer by the day. We had a great 4th of July weekend and then it was Monday, the day I had been waiting for. I was a wreck. Could I count on the fact that Liz would show up again? What if she didn't? Of course, I had asked her nicely countless times – could she please come?

We arrived at Kathryn's, and again, my anxiety left as soon as I entered her studio and sat down on her couch. She again took my hand and proceeded to tell me that someone was either moving into my house or out of it. Yes, I said, someone is moving out. Anna, my "other daughter" was moving out to go to college. "This looks like a good move for her," she said. "And, it frees you up quite a bit."

Then Kathryn asked me, "What else would you like to know?"

"I really came to connect with someone close to me. We did that last time I was here. That is the real reason I am here."

"Tell me the name of the person you want to connect with," she said.

"Elizabeth," I said.

"Is this a daughter?"

"Yes."

"Okay, it's a little girl that's coming through."

"Yes, she came through little last time I was here."

"She didn't die that young, but she was a teenager when she died."

Amazing. Kathryn was giving me the exact same information as she had the first time I had come.

"Liz says that the last time she came in she said a lot of things to you that she hopes you remember. "

"Yes, she told me that she loved me."

"Yes," Kathryn said, "if she could say anything to you, that would be it, just how much she loves you."

"Does she still check in at our house much?" I asked.

"Yes, but not as much. But she does come for major family events."

"Well, we just had a major family event about 3 weeks ago."

"Yes," Kathryn said, "you had what Liz calls a big party."

"Yes, that's right," I said.

"She said it was a big party and it was outside. And most of the people at the party she hadn't seen since her funeral. She sat on the grass and watched Joey. He was carrying on with some kind of antics, and she thought it was funny."

Joey, Joey, I wondered . . . who was Joey? My mind was blank.

Sue spoke up: "Joey is Darcy's son."

Oh, yes. How could I forget? My cousin Darcy – her son was Joey. Now I remembered, they were playing basketball on the driveway and he was walking around being funny.

"You have to remember," Kathryn said, "she is looking at this as about a 6- or 7-year-old child; so that is what would have interested her."

"Yes," I said, "Joey is 6 years old. But why is she 6 or 7 when she was 20 when she died?"

"Because," Kathryn said, "she has chosen to go back and be able to play and have fun as a child does."

"Will she always be that young?" I asked. "As long as she wants to be," Kathryn said. "It is her choice."

"Fascinating. What does she do?"

"She plays."

Oh, brother. What was more amazing, Liz talked about the picture boards that we had in the garage at Anna's party. She was so happy that we had included pictures of her.

I told Kathryn that I thought there was a possibility that some of Liz's high school friends may come to see her to talk to Liz.

"Is there a Kathy?" Kathryn asked.

Again, my mind was blank. I couldn't think of a single friend named Kathy.

"She went to grade school with her."

I still drew a blank. It took about 3 or 4 more days until it hit me. It wasn't Kathy – it was Cassie. I bet that was what Liz was trying to say, "Cassie." I emailed Kathryn, saying I thought Liz was saying Cassie; that was who she gave her first sign to.

Kathryn answered me, saying, "That could very well be. Sometimes I have a hard time hearing the difference between words such as Cassie and Kathy."

Wow, another validation of this wonderful gift of spirit communication.

I was on a high for a long time after that visit. It left no doubt in my mind whatsoever. Liz was there for Anna's graduation party. She described it perfectly. The four of us were still a family.

A good friend from work lost her father very unexpectedly a few months previously. Her mother and most of her family were going on a trip to Hawaii that her dad was to have gone on as well. For some reason I felt compelled to send her an email. "You might not believe this," I said, "and if you don't, that's okay. Just pretend you didn't get this. But, you might want to watch for signs from your dad. I have received several from Liz and I would be happy to tell you about them if you want to hear."

"Yes, I do believe and I would like to hear more," Joan emailed me back.

Oh, wow. I get to tell my story. I wanted to tell someone for the longest time. But how do you tell a story like this without people thinking you have gone over the edge?

The next day when those around me were off to lunch, the opportunity presented itself. Joan came to my desk and I told her about the signs we had received and about my visits with Kathryn.

"Wow, that's amazing," she said. "I remember seeing that story about her on the news." She said that at some point she might want to go see Kathryn. "Will you come with me?"

"You don't have to ask me twice. Of course, I will," I said.

The month of September had arrived – the dreaded month. I had been thinking about it since about June. Wondering, how would I get through this horrible month?

First we have her birthday on the 12th. She would have been 21. Well, that would have been some party, I thought to myself. She would have been legal. It was a day I had waited a long time for. Now, it meant nothing. Eight days later we would mark the first anniversary of her death. I was positive she would give me a sign at some point during that month. After all, it was a big, important month. Surely she would come through for me.

Her birthday came. Roger, my dad, my two brothers and my nephew went up north on a guy's fishing trip. That left my mom and me. Sue, I said, can you please come down for the weekend? We needed to do something fun that weekend. My niece Maddy was in a water ski tournament on Saturday in Shoreview. We would go to the cities, and we would pick up Anna at her dorm – Sue and my mom hadn't seen it yet – then we'll go watch Maddy ski. That will be fun. We'll eat out; we'll do a little shopping; sounds good; a girl's day.

And we did all that, plus a little more. It turned into a "Liz" day. And it was good. "We've never seen the plaque that was placed at Bailey Hall in honor of the three," everyone told me. "Can you show us?" Of course, I said. So we go to Bailey Hall and stand and gaze at the picture of Liz, Brian and Amanda on the outside wall. "We've also never seen the tree that was planted at the park across the street from Liz's house. Can we see that too?" Well sure, why not. And we do. And it is fine.

We dropped Anna off at her dorm and headed home. It had been a good day. I could feel that Liz was pleased. We were remembering her. The next day was her birthday – the day I had dreaded. But still, it was a good day. I put flowers on the altar at church in her memory. Two of my closest friends didn't want me to be alone, so they came and picked me up in Jeanne's convertible and we drove to a nearby town festival. We walked around the various shops and flea markets. We did a lot of looking and laughing. It was fun. They helped me get through the day. That's what friends are for. I'm so lucky I have such good ones. It was a great day. I had never ridden in a convertible, and the wind blew our hair every which way, but we didn't care.

But still, not a sign from Liz. I guess she's waiting for the first anniversary of her death, I told myself. We planned a get-together with Brian and Amanda's parents, and we would host a picnic for the roommates and other college friends in the park across from the house. Again, I had dreaded this day for a long time, but it dawned sunny and mild. We spent time with the other parents and shared our memories and our sadness. Then we went to the park and set up our food, and to our surprise over 30 kids showed up to help us remember. It was awesome and wonderful. Brian's dad Rich went over to the house. It had been remodeled, and new kids were living there. They knew that this was "the house" and they graciously allowed those of us who wanted to, a chance to go in.

"Do you want to?" Roger asked. I didn't know. Should I subject myself to that? I wasn't sure. But, I thought, if I don't go now, I probably would never have the chance again.

Okay, I said, I'll go. It was painful, but do-able. The porch where the fire started was completely gone. But the rest of the house was the same, at least structure-wise.

All of the rooms were the same configuration, but had new plaster and flooring. The kitchen had new appliances and new cupboards. Wow, I thought, I wish the house could have been this nice when Liz was here.

We started up the same narrow stairway to the upstairs. The first door was Fik's old room. Then the next door was Liz and Amanda's room. Again, it looked as I remembered it, only much newer. I gazed at the window that had been right above Liz's bed. I remembered what I had thought on that day over a year ago. Even a window so close, and it hadn't made a difference, I thought.

But, I felt triumphant as we left the house. It was like a battle I had conquered. I had survived the day; it had been a good day and I had even returned to the scene of death and destruction, and survived. Life was good.

But still, not a single sign from my girl. I was puzzled, kind of annoyed, and very worried.

Maybe this is it, I thought. It's been a year; she knows I'm doing pretty well, all things considered. Even if I never get another thing from her, I have to be satisfied with all that she's given me. I had to admit that was true. But, still I wanted more. And, I was so afraid I wasn't going to get it. As the next couple of weeks went by I grew more and more despondent. I even skipped going to work one day and just sat at home and felt sorry for myself.

The next day, I thought, get a grip, Kim; this is crazy. You just have to accept this and get on with your life. I went back to work. I emailed Julie and told her how sad I was. I think this is it, I told her. I don't think Liz is going to check in any more. I sent off the email to Julie and less than a minute later I got an email from Joan. What are you doing on October 14th, she asked me? Right away, I knew what she meant: Am I going with you to Maple Grove?

Oh my goodness, I'm going back to Kathryn's. In the span of a couple of minutes my disposition had changed. I emailed Kathryn. "I'm coming with Joan for her session, could I have about 15 minutes to talk to my girl?" I asked. Sure, no problem, Kathryn replied.

The next weekend Anna came home from college. I bemoaned the fact that I hadn't received a sign from Liz in September, as I was so sure I would. Suddenly Anna said, "Oh, I forgot to tell you this. Remember the day before Liz's birthday when you came to the cities and we had such a great day? Yes, I remember. Well, after you dropped me off I was so tired so I took a nap. Only Liz woke me up. She just kept yelling my name, really loud until I woke up."

Oh wow – she had come through after all; it just wasn't to me. "Oh, Anna, why didn't you call and tell me this?" I asked.

"Oh, I forgot."

"How on earth can you forget something so important?" But, that's my Anna. Nothing much fazes her. I just couldn't believe it. My girl was still alive and well and keeping in touch.

It was October 13th, and Joan wasn't at work. I was a little worried. I hoped it was nothing serious and we could still make her session tomorrow. I found that Joan had left me a message earlier in the day: "I'm really sick, and I can't go tomorrow. Can you call Kathryn for me?"

Sure, I said. But, I can't not go now . . . my heart is set on it and I've got my list of questions.

I called Kathryn, saying Joan is ill and can't keep her appointment tomorrow, but could I take her spot?

"Well, of course," Kathryn said, "but you don't have to, I mean it would be fine for me to have the morning free. After all, it's only been a couple of months since you were here; do you really think you need to come?"

"Oh yes," I said, "I have lots to talk about."

"Okay, that's great. I'll see you tomorrow."

I told Julie of this new development. "You know you don't like to drive," she said. "Do you want me to take you?"

"Well, sure, if you want to."

So it is set. I still get to go, and I don't have to drive.

Once again, the butterflies in my stomach were flying in formation. Would Liz show up? I was always so fearful that she wouldn't. But, I was ready to talk, to plead, even to beg. Please, please, don't leave me. Don't stop connecting with me. I knew, though, if I never got another thing from her, I had to accept it and I had to be satisfied. After all, she had already given me so much.

But I didn't even have to plead or beg. As soon as I sat down on the couch, Kathryn gave me a little blue bag with something in it. "Here," she said. "Liz asked me to give you this." Nervously, my fingers pulled the strings apart to open it. I reached in and pulled out a long slender crystal on a small string.

Kathryn told me, "This is a pendulum and I'm going to show you how to use it. Then whenever you need to talk to Liz you can. Hold it between your fingers," she instructed. "Now take your other hand and make it be still."

I held it and made it stop moving.

"Okay, now say, 'Show me yes.'"

"Should I say it out loud or in my mind?" I asked.

"Either way is fine."

So out loud I said, "Show me yes." And I watched. I am not moving my hand that is holding the pendulum, but slowly it starts to rock towards me. That means yes.

"Now, tell it to show you no," Kathryn said.

I steadied it again so it was not moving. "Show me no," I said. Once again, slowly it began to move, only this time it moved from left to right, totally different from the yes command. That means no. Wow. I was not moving my hand at all.

"Do you see this, Julie?" I said.

"Yes," she said, but Kathryn encouraged her to move in for a closer look.

"Now let's ask some questions. Ask if Liz is here."

I took a deep breath. "Liz, are you here?" The crystal started to move vigorously in the yes motion. Oh, my God. I can hardly keep it together.

"Are you okay?" Kathryn asked.

Yes, yes, I am more than okay. But I am exhausted. I am hoping we don't have to do the whole session this way. I put the pendulum down. "Do I have to keep using it now?" I asked.

"No, of course not."

Before I knew it, my session was once again over. But I was filled with joy and happiness. I now had a way to talk to my girl whenever I wanted to. I came home and that night started to write down as many yes-or-no questions as I could think of. I would use the pendulum daily and ask Liz questions until I ran out. I'm sure after about day three she was getting annoyed. I could no longer think of new questions so I kept asking her the same things again and again.

"Liz," I said, "every Tuesday we'll talk, okay?" But Tuesday would come and I really didn't have much to say. She was there, but we didn't have anything to talk about – at least that could be answered with either yes or no.

This isn't working. I decide I will only use it when I feel compelled to. To date, that has worked well for me. Holidays are difficult and it is so reassuring to know that even though I can't see or feel her, she is there on those days. I know she is, my pendulum tells me so.

Joan recovered and was back at work. I was not going to push. If she really wants to go see Kathryn, I figured, she will make a new appointment when she is ready.

Again, Joan emailed me. "Will you still go with me if I make a new appointment?"

"Of course I will."

Joan called Kathryn and set up a new date, November 15th. "Is Kim coming?" Kathryn asked.

"Yes, she is," Joan said.

"Okay," I told Liz, "I'm going to Joan's session and I will just be an observer. I am going to leave it up to you. It's your choice if you want to crash Joan's session. I will wait for your cue."

It was fun to be an observer for a change, but I kept waiting for Kathryn to tell me that Liz was there and had something to tell me. She didn't. But, Kathryn was able to connect Joan to her father and describe him and the circumstances of his death in enough detail for Joan to know that she was indeed for real. "That is some amazing gift you have," Joan said. "I don't know that I would want it, though."

Kathryn agreed. "It is difficult sometimes," she admitted.

Yes, I think, I'm sure she would sometimes wonder if people really liked her for her, or if they pretended to like her because of her amazing intuitive abilities. Kind of like a celebrity, in a way. How do they know who their real friends are? Can they separate the intuitive Kathryn from the person Kathryn? I would like to think I could. I sure would like to have the chance to try.

Someday, I hope it will work out so that we can do something together that is just as friends, and we will leave our intuition at home for the day. That is a goal I will work towards, I decide.

So after that November day, I stayed in contact with Kathryn as often as I could, and I tried not to be a pest. After all, she led a busy, active life. She didn't need me. But, I sure did need her.

I love to cook and bake when I have the time. My oversized body is proof of that. What can I do for Kathryn, I thought? She has done so much for me. What can I do that she can't? Suddenly I remembered her saying at one of my sessions that she didn't cook. Well, if she didn't cook, she most likely didn't bake either. I would soon be making my Christmas cookies for the upcoming holidays. I decided I would send some to her.

That was my new mission, and it gave me something to think about and look forward to doing. It would feel so good to do something nice for someone who had done so much for me.

I put the cookies in a shoebox and packed them with care so they would arrive whole and not broken in a million pieces. I threw in our Christmas card that had our family picture on it. I had chosen our picture this year. It was one that we had taken of the three of us at Anna's graduation party. In the background were the picture boards that Liz had so enjoyed. It symbolized that we were still a family.

We had survived the unimaginable and were going on with our lives with smiles. Liz was a part of it as well. Four snowmen adorned the side of the card. You are included, my precious girl. We are still a family of four. The world saw us only as three, but I knew better.

Roger and I were celebrating our 25th wedding anniversary on December 29, 2004. We wanted to go somewhere for the occasion, but were unsure as to where or when.

At first we thought of Las Vegas. It could be just a quick trip and wouldn't cost that much. We could go on our anniversary, we thought. Then we learned that our company would be closing our plant for a week in January. They were prone to do that on occasion – "to save money," they would tell us. It was fine with us. We had both been there for over 30 years and we had plenty of vacation time to use.

Roger was on the computer looking at Vegas options and somehow ended up on a website showing the beauty of Jamaica. "Look at this, Kim," he said. I love the ocean so I was very attracted to Jamaica. I had never been there but the pictures looked wonderful. "Oh, can we go there?" It didn't take much convincing and it was settled; we were going to Jamaica for a week. I could hardly contain my excitement.

Christmas was over and we had once again survived. It was a little easier this year. I guess we all knew what to expect. And, of course, I knew Liz was with us because my pendulum told me so.

I emailed Kathryn – did she have a good Christmas? I did, I told her, adding, "And guess what, Roger and I are going to Jamaica on January 2nd."

Kathryn emailed me back. Her holidays had been good too, she said. And, she very much enjoyed the treats I had sent her. She went on to say she was happy to hear we were going to Jamaica. She had been there many times, and it was a mystical island full of beauty and enjoyment.

It was fun to exchange emails with her about another subject other than Liz or intuition. She gave me some hints on what to do and where to go and told me I would have a wonderful trip. I even knew that would be true.

Roger and I did have a fabulous time. It seemed fitting to mark such a momentous occasion.

I'm so lucky, I thought to myself. I love Roger so much. I was disappointed he didn't share my enthusiasm for signs from Liz, but I had made peace with it.

I just wished I could tell him about my visits to Kathryn. I thought it would help him if he would only listen. And, I don't like keeping secrets from him. I felt I had to tell him at some point, but I just couldn't do it. I brought along James Van Praagh's book, *Talking to Heaven*, to read on the beach. I didn't hide it, but laid it out in full view on the table in our room. Surely he must see it there, I thought.

I read it every day on the beach. I wasn't going to sneak around. Maybe this would spark a discussion I thought. He hadn't brought any reading materials along and by the fourth day was looking for something to read. I had long since finished the book and was on to another. "Why don't you read this," I told him. "I think it would do you some good." He looked at it, and opened the pages for a couple of minutes. "No, I don't think so," he said. Well I tried, I thought to myself.

The week sped by and we were headed home. It had been a marvelous week. Liz hadn't made her presence known, but that was okay. I kept looking for something, though. I fantasized about a mysterious man that I would encounter on the beach.

He would be wearing a trench coat and have a hat on his head that would shade his eyes. We would meet and he would say, "Liz says to tell you Hello." Then he would walk past me. I would turn to look at him, and he would be gone. After all, this was a mysterious island, Kathryn had told me. But, it didn't happen.

When I got home, I couldn't resist. I had to email Kathryn and tell her what a fabulous time we had.

"That's great, I knew you would," she replied. "I got an email the other day from a woman who said she had talked to someone about me while on a plane to Jamaica. I bet that was you."

"Wow, I wish I could take credit for that, Kathryn, but I can't. The only person sitting next to me was Roger."

"That's fascinating," Kathryn emailed back. "I wonder whom she was talking to?"

Then Kathryn said she needed to ask a favor of me. "I'm including testimonials from some of my clients in my new book. Would you consider writing one for me?"

"You don't have to ask me twice," I answered her. "I love to write and I would be honored."

"Whenever you get around to it," Kathryn said, "but maybe in the next week or two?"

Once I started to write it, I couldn't put it down until I was done. How could I sum up in a couple of paragraphs how much this woman had helped me? I wrote it and nipped and tucked it until I was satisfied. "Here it is, Kathryn, do with it as you please. Thanks for asking; it was fun."

Once again, I'm amazed at where my life has taken me; who would have thought? I still have to pinch myself sometimes to see if it is real. But it is. It is my world and I so love it.

But, I have learned some hard lessons. Not everyone embraces intuition or spirit communication. They think it is baloney and that everyone who believes in it is a little off. Why, I'm married to a huge skeptic myself, but that's okay. I love him anyway. Everyone has a choice, I remind myself. I can't force anyone to believe my story. I can only tell it, and those who believe it will, and for those who don't it is okay. That is their choice.

I often think now, would I change anything if I could? You bet I would. I would have wanted Liz to stay. I truly believe that somehow we would have worked things out. The world would have been a better place if she had stayed. I think she would have made a difference to many people.

But I respect and understand her decision to leave. She has made me a better person because of it. She opened a new door for me that I never thought I would walk through. And, she has learned and grown from her experience here on earth, and she continues to learn, grow, and love in her new world, just as I do here in mine.

So again, we are still connected. It's not the relationship I thought we would have, but the important thing is that we still have a relationship. And, it really is no longer a mother-daughter relationship. It has moved to a new level. She now sees me in a new light. When she was here, I was simply her mother. I took care of her and provided for her needs. She did not see that I was a person outside of being her mother; I had goals, wants, and desires that were separate from being a mother.

In the same way, I no longer have to mother her. She can now stand on her own and function as a whole person. I no longer need to worry about her. We now can relate to each other in a new and different way – as souls who are forever joined. And one day, I will walk through the veil that still separates us and we will be completely united. I look forward to that day. But for now, I am so very happy with what I have been given. It is a blessing and a sacred trust that will not be broken.

And the source of it all is God; a God who is there for each of us. Who loves us more than any of us can ever fathom. And, what he does for one, he can do for all. I am not a special person, set apart from the rest. I am an ordinary soul. I want to be an ordinary soul. In fact, I take pride in being an ordinary soul. If God can do this for me, he can do this for you as well. You just need to talk to him and ask for what you want. Set your intentions, and be watchful and accepting of what you receive. And above all, always remember that love is the key to all things.

I still continue to see Kathryn. In fact, I have started on a new journey with her. I am now a student in her Intuitive Mastery Program. My goal is to learn to connect with Liz, my Guides and Angels in new and different ways. I want to help others, especially parents who have lost a child; and I believe that with the help of Liz, my Guides, my God, and Kathryn, it is a winning combination. I don't know where this journey will take me, but I am ready to embark on it.

I have been given so much. "To those whom much is given, much is expected," I remind myself.

So, this is my story. I've struggled with how to end it because it doesn't have an ending. It still continues today and will go on tomorrow and all the days that follow. I will leave you with the thought I began with, which is love. It truly does not die, but is eternal. The bond we all share with those we love is never broken, not even by death. My story is a living, breathing testament to that. I hope that thought comforts you as much as it does me, and I wish you a happy, safe and love-filled journey.

In Loving Memory of
Elizabeth Jean Wencl

September 12, 1983 – September 20, 2003

By: Kim Wencl

As I am putting together the final stories for this book, I am so grateful for the new friends that I have met. It has been another year since my mom Beverly passed away. The book is now in its completion and ironically enough, that ending has landed on February 15th, 2007. It was one year ago today that I had the idea for this book, and the day I began searching for the stories like mine and two years to the day since my mom passed away. It has been an amazing search, to say the least. I truly believe that when I began putting this book together, the stories that I received from people I didn't even know were exactly the perfect fit. It wasn't easy beginning a search for something that you were particular about. The biggest of all is being content. Each one of my new friends felt the exact same contentment that I did with my mom. Our miracles and signs were different, but the overwhelming feeling of "everything is okay" was with all of us.

There were so many different venues that I chose to begin my quest, and I would like to thank a few websites that allowed me to post an article looking for stories. Leo Pond from unexplainedmysteries .com gave me a front row seat on his website and I was able to meet two great people from that site. I also went to the Lung Cancer Support Group at lchelp.org where there is an incredible message board where you will meet so many other people who have felt the same pain, laughter, anger and fear as you have. Last but not least, castleofspirits.com had two wonderful stories to share as well. I would also like to thank Kim, Laura, Ann, Annie, Lilian, Connie, Lisa, Eva, Patty and Sharon for making me cry again, because I had to proofread all of the stories before I sent them to my buddy Nowick Gray to edit this book.

I swear, I truly feel as though I'm not alone, and neither is my mom. She is standing up in Heaven with her new friends as well; as I'm sure they had a hand in bringing all of us together. No matter how much the tears flow through the pain you could feel through this book, the contentment is just as strong, and that was the purpose.